11	12	13	14	15	16	17	18
							2 **He** HELIUM 4.003 P. 24
		5 **B** BORON 10.81 P. 27	6 **C** CARBON 12.011 P. 28	7 **N** NITROGEN 14.007 P. 30	8 **O** OXYGEN 15.999 P. 32	9 **F** FLUORINE 18.998 P. 34	10 **Ne** NEON 20.180 P. 35
		13 **Al** ALUMINUM 26.982 P. 39	14 **Si** SILICON 28.085 P. 42	15 **P** PHOSPHORUS 30.974 P. 43	16 **S** SULFUR 32.06 P. 45	17 **Cl** CHLORINE 35.45 P. 46	18 **Ar** ARGON 39.95 P. 48
29 **Cu** COPPER 63.546 P. 68	30 **Zn** ZINC 65.38 P. 69	31 **Ga** GALLIUM 69.723 P. 70	32 **Ge** GERMANIUM 72.630 P. 71	33 **As** ARSENIC 74.922 P. 72	34 **Se** SELENIUM 78.971 P. 73	35 **Br** BROMINE 79.904 P. 74	36 **Kr** KRYPTON 83.798 P. 76
47 **Ag** SILVER 107.868 P. 89	48 **Cd** CADMIUM 112.414 P. 90	49 **In** INDIUM 114.818 P. 91	50 **Sn** TIN 118.710 P. 92	51 **Sb** ANTIMONY 121.760 P. 93	52 **Te** TELLURIUM 127.60 P. 94	53 **I** IODINE 126.904 P. 95	54 **Xe** XENON 131.293 P. 96
79 **Au** GOLD 196.967 P. 115	80 **Hg** MERCURY 200.592 P. 116	81 **Tl** THALLIUM 204.38 P. 118	82 **Pb** LEAD 207.2 P. 119	83 **Bi** BISMUTH 208.980 P. 120	84 **Po** POLONIUM (209) P. 121	85 **At** ASTATINE (210) P. 122	86 **Rn** RADON (222) P. 122
111 **Rg** ROENTGENIUM (282) P. 136	112 **Cn** COPERNICIUM (285) P. 136	113 **Nh** NIHONIUM (286) P. 136	114 **Fl** FLEROVIUM (289) P. 136	115 **Mc** MOSCOVIUM (289) P. 136	116 **Lv** LIVERMORIUM (293) P. 136	117 **Ts** TENNESSINE (294) P. 136	118 **Og** OGANESSON (294) P. 136

65 **Tb** TERBIUM 158.925 P. 104	66 **Dy** DYSPROSIUM 162.500 P. 105	67 **Ho** HOLMIUM 164.930 P. 105	68 **Er** ERBIUM 167.259 P. 106	69 **Tm** THULIUM 168.934 P. 106	70 **Yb** YTTERBIUM 173.045 P. 107	71 **Lu** LUTETIUM 174.967 P. 107
97 **Bk** BERKELIUM (247) P. 133	98 **Cf** CALIFORNIUM (251) P. 133	99 **Es** EINSTEINIUM (252) P. 134	100 **Fm** FERMIUM (257) P. 134	101 **Md** MENDELEVIUM (258) P. 136	102 **No** NOBELIUM (259) P. 136	103 **Lr** LAWRENCIUM (266) P. 136

THE PERIODIC TABLE OF THE ELEMENTS

HOW TO READ THIS TABLE:

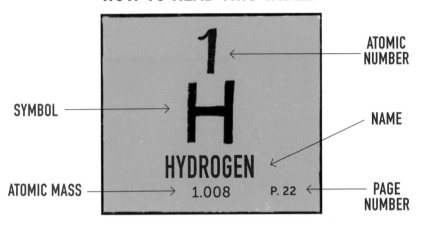

ATOMIC NUMBER

SYMBOL

NAME

ATOMIC MASS

PAGE NUMBER

1

H

HYDROGEN

1.008   P. 22

ALKALI METALS

ALKALINE EARTH METALS

LANTHANOIDS

ACTINOIDS

TRANSITION METALS

POST-TRANSITION METALS

METALLOIDS

REACTIVE NONMETALS

NOBLE GASES

UNKNOWN

PERIOD

		1	2
1		1 **H** HYDROGEN 1.008 P. 22	
2		3 **Li** LITHIUM 6.94 P. 25	4 **Be** BERYLLIUM 9.012 P. 26
3		11 **Na** SODIUM 22.990 P. 36	12 **Mg** MAGNESIUM 24.305 P. 37
4		19 **K** POTASSIUM 39.098 P. 49	20 **Ca** CALCIUM 40.078 P. 50	2. S.. SCAN.. 44...
5		37 **Rb** RUBIDIUM 85.468 P. 77	38 **Sr** STRONTIUM 87.62 P. 78	3.. **Y** YTTR.. 88..
6		55 **Cs** CESIUM 132.905 P. 97	56 **Ba** BARIUM 137.327 P. 98	5.. **L...** LANTH.. 138..
7		87 **Fr** FRANCIUM (223) P. 123	88 **Ra** RADIUM (226) P. 124	8.. **A...** ACTI.. (2..

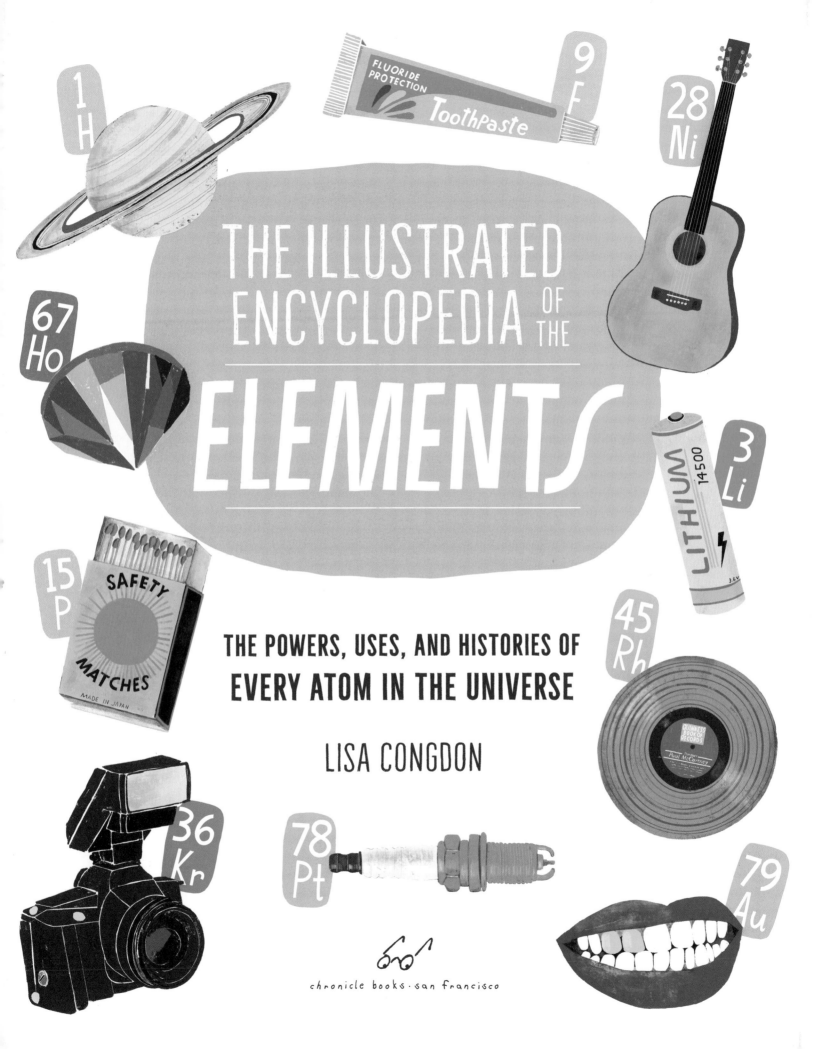

THE ILLUSTRATED ENCYCLOPEDIA OF THE ELEMENTS

THE POWERS, USES, AND HISTORIES OF
EVERY ATOM IN THE UNIVERSE

LISA CONGDON

chronicle books · san francisco

Library of Congress Cataloging-in-Publication Data available.

ISBN 978-1-4521-6159-4

Manufactured in China.

Design by Jay Marvel and Patrick T. O'Hay.
Typeset in Capita and Sofia Pro Soft.
The illustrations in this book were rendered in
gouache and edited digitally.

10 9 8 7 6 5 4 3 2 1

Chronicle Books LLC
680 Second Street
San Francisco, California 94107

Chronicle Books—we see things differently. Become part of our
community at www.chroniclekids.com.

▲▲▲▲▲▲▲▲▲▲▲▲▲▲▲▲▲▲▲▲▲

FOR MY SISTER STEPHANIE, WITHOUT WHOM THIS
BOOK WOULD NOT EXIST.
IT IS AS MUCH YOURS AS IT IS MINE.
I LOVE YOU. – L. C.

▲▲▲▲▲▲▲▲▲▲▲▲▲▲▲▲▲▲▲▲▲

CONTENTS

INTRODUCTION

When I was a little girl, I would sit at the kitchen table and watch my father work. After dinner he would write equations on graph paper. I knew he was a scientist, but the exquisite handwritten equations were all I knew about what my father did in his career as a physicist. At that time, I was intrigued, but science seemed mysterious and complicated to me. It wasn't until I became an elementary school teacher in my early twenties and began teaching various science subjects to my students that science came to life for me. I loved learning with my students about the elements that make up the universe. Years later, I am no longer a teacher, but a professional artist, and making this book is a way for me to use my interest in science and my love for drawing pictures to bring the elements of the periodic table to life for kids and adults alike. Both art and science are enormously creative fields. Both require openness to innovation and rigorous discipline. Both force us to experiment with our ideas in the zone where our minds and hands come together. Artists and scientists dive deep into their subject matter and study things, such as people, culture, history, religion, and mythology. From these investigations, we have the opportunity to transform information into something new.

The periodic table is a catalog of everything tangible in our world. Everything we touch, eat, drink, and breathe is made up of the elements. Some elements are so common that they are part of our everyday vocabulary, such as oxygen, aluminum, and silver. Conversely, some elements, such as yttrium, antimony, and moscovium, are so obscure that their names and uses are unknown to many of us.

At first glance, the periodic table of elements might look like a boring, uninspiring chart. And if you look at it simply as a series of boxes, it *will* be pretty boring. However, if you dive into the table, you will begin to understand that it is not boring at all, nor is it mysterious or random, as I once thought. It is a chart that is organized by predictable truths about the way everything on Earth is built, starting with tiny atoms and even tinier protons, neutrons, and electrons.

With a few exceptions, nearly every element on the periodic table has a purpose in our world. Even some of the most poisonous or dangerous elements have compelling roles in our lives. Some elements keep our bodies working efficiently. Others kill deadly cancer cells and help us detect harmful diseases. Still others are mined from rocks for bridges, buildings, and airplanes. We are constantly finding new ways to use the elements in technology, health care, and the generation of energy to fuel our world.

If you are a person who likes to ask *why* and *how*, you might already be a scientist. In this book, I will introduce you to the dynamic and fascinating elements, the roles they play in our lives, and how they function in the world, as well as some of the compelling stories about the people who discovered them. Dmitri Mendeleev, the guy who organized the periodic table back in 1869, was a curious young person, just like you! Every discovery starts with curiosity.

▲ ▲ ▲ ▲ ▲ ▲ ▲ ▲

WHAT IS AN ELEMENT?

Everything in the world that you see and feel—your body, the ground you are standing on, the book you are holding, the stars in the sky—is made of elements. There are 118 known elements in the universe. More than 90 are naturally occurring on Earth, and the remainder are human-made. In turn, the elements are made up of gazillions of tiny atoms. A single element is a pure substance that is made from one kind of atom, and can't be broken down into any smaller, simpler substances. For example, the element hydrogen contains only hydrogen atoms, and the element silver contains only silver atoms.

ALL ABOUT ATOMS

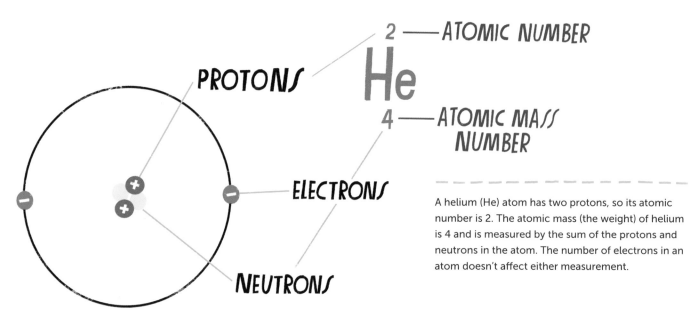

2 — ATOMIC NUMBER

He

4 — ATOMIC MASS NUMBER

PROTONS

ELECTRONS

NEUTRONS

A helium (He) atom has two protons, so its atomic number is 2. The atomic mass (the weight) of helium is 4 and is measured by the sum of the protons and neutrons in the atom. The number of electrons in an atom doesn't affect either measurement.

Small Wonder

Atoms are so tiny that they are too small to see except with extremely powerful microscopes! Every atom has a dense center called a nucleus. Forming the nucleus are two kinds of particles: protons, which have a positive electrical charge, and neutrons, which have no charge. Bound to the nucleus are one or more electrons, which are particles with a negative charge. Scientists used to describe atoms as tiny solar systems, with the electrons orbiting around the nucleus like planets around the sun, but atoms are a lot hazier than that. If you imagined the tiny nucleus as a pea, it would be centered in a football stadium–size cloud that includes the electrons. We can't be sure where the electrons are because they are impossible to pin down.

Protons, We've Got Your Number

All atoms have at least one proton in their core. And protons determine an atom's uniqueness. The number of protons determines the element. For example, hydrogen has just one proton. No other element is made up of atoms that contain one proton. For this reason, we list the different elements by their number of protons. This is called the atomic number. The atomic number determines where the element sits on the periodic table of elements, the organized chart of all of the elements that have been discovered.

Neither Here nor There

Neutrons have neither a positive nor a negative charge. No matter how many neutrons are in an atom, they do not affect the charge. However, neutrons do affect the mass (the weight) of an atom. The atomic mass is the sum of all the protons and neutrons in the element.

Electrons in Orbit

In addition to protons and neutrons, all atoms have electrons. Electrons are negatively charged particles that orbit the space surrounding the positively charged nuclear core. These orbits are called electron shells. Each electron shell has a different energy level, with the electron shells farthest from the nucleus having the highest energy levels. This outermost shell is known as the valence shell, and the electrons found in it are called valence electrons. The number of electrons in the valence shell determines the atom's reactivity or tendency to form chemical bonds with other atoms. Atoms are most stable and least likely to be reactive when their valence shell is full of all the electrons it can hold.

In Balance

Neutral atoms have an equal number of protons and electrons, and the number of protons and neutrons is usually the same—but sometimes not. Adding or removing neutrons to an atom makes an isotope: a heavier or lighter version of that same element with the same chemical properties. Changing the number of electrons in an atom also does not change the type of element it is, but it does change its chemical behavior (the atom is no longer neutral in charge and is now called an ion). But adding a proton? Suddenly you've got an entirely new element with—you guessed it—a new atomic number.

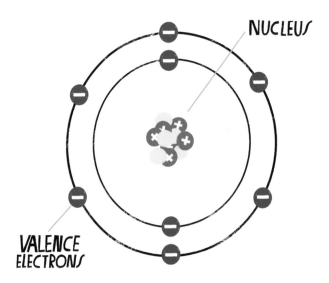

NUCLEUS

VALENCE ELECTRONS

- An atom is about one angstrom in diameter, which is about 100,000 times smaller than a red blood cell.

- Electrons travel at a speed of 1,367 miles (2,200 kilometres) per second, and at this speed they could orbit Earth in 18 seconds.

- 99.99999999999 percent of an atom is empty space.

- A single human hair is about as thick as one hundred thousand atoms.

- Make a fist. It contains about 15,000,000,000,000,000,000, 000,000 (that's 15 *septillion*) atoms! If each atom in your fist were the size of a marble, your fist would be the size of Earth.

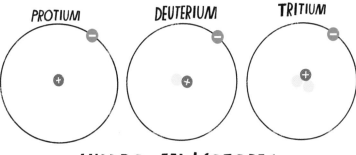

PROTIUM DEUTERIUM TRITIUM

HYDROGEN ISOTOPES

COMPOUNDS

Anytime two atoms join together, they make a molecule. Everything around us is made up of molecules. When atoms from two or more different elements bind together, the molecule is a compound. The chemical bond is so strong that the atoms from the different elements all behave like a single substance. Compounds are not simply mixtures or blends, but a bind that happens at the atomic level. Sometimes an element will lose traits when it is bound in a compound. An element that is reactive on its own (meaning it will release energy in a chemical reaction with another element), like sodium (Na), can become nonreactive when it binds with another element like chlorine (Cl), forming sodium chloride (NaCl), which is everyday table salt.

All compounds have a definite composition. For example, a compound you may have heard about before is H_2O, or water. Water always has two hydrogen atoms and one oxygen atom. If you take away one of the hydrogen atoms, it is no longer water. While we have only 118 elements in the periodic table, there are millions and millions of compound combinations that are each unique.

Alloys Versus Compounds

Alloys are not compounds. An alloy is a mixture of metals, or a metal and another element. Brass is an alloy of copper and zinc, which are both metals. Steel is an alloy of iron (a metal), carbon (a nonmetal), and sometimes other elements. The alloy components are usually melted at very high temperatures, mixed, and allowed to cool to a solid alloy. In general, alloys are stronger and more durable than their individual components. Unlike compounds, alloys do not have chemical bonds between the elements.

COMMON COMPOUNDS

Some compounds you might know by their common names:

Liquid bleach: $NaClO$

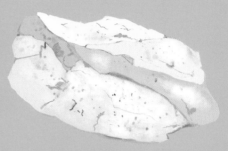

Marble: $CaCO_3$

BAKING ★ SODA

NET WT 16 OZ

Baking soda: $NaHCO_3$

91%

ISOPROPYL ALCOHOL

WARNING FLAMMABLE

16 FL OUNCES

Rubbing alcohol: $(CH_3)_2CHOH$

Milk of Magnesia

16 FL. OZ

Milk of magnesia: $Mg(OH)_2$

SUGAR
PURE GRANULATED

Sugar: $C_{12}H_{22}O_{11}$

Table Salt: $NaCl$

STATES OF MATTER

All elements can exist in three different states of matter: solid, liquid, or gas. We use "room temperature"—a comfortable temperature of about 70° Fahrenheit (21° Celsius)—as our consistent point of reference. At room temperature, the majority of the elements are solid, eleven are gas, and two are liquid. Elements change from one state to another through heating and cooling. When an element changes from one state to another, the number of atoms remains the same, but they arrange themselves in different ways.

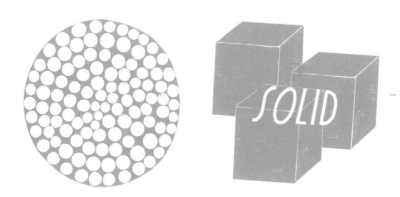

When an element is in solid form, atoms are attracted to each other and locked into a tight position. Solids keep their shape and have a fixed volume (volume is how much space an object takes up). While some solids are soft and flexible, they are still solid.

When an element is in liquid form, the atoms move around and their attraction loosens. Liquids take the shape of the container they are in, but their volume remains fixed.

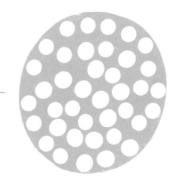

When an element is in a gas form, the atoms are weakly attracted to each other and move in different directions. A gas will fill any container, no matter how large or small it is.

ALCHEMY AND ANCIENT CHEMISTRY

L ong before the periodic table was developed, humans attempted to understand the unique and distinct substances that comprised everything in the known universe. *What are these essential elements?* Many ancient cultures, like the Babylonians, Chinese, and Egyptians, developed an idea of simple groups: wood, fire, earth, metal, water, and so on. The ancient Greeks synthesized the world into just four elements: earth, water, fire, and air. This theory became *elemental* to Western thought for 2,000 years. The four elements were used to describe not only objects in the seen world, but also the temperaments a person might experience and physical sensations in the body, called the four humors. Maintaining the balance of the four elements/humors was thought to be essential not just to the natural world, but also to a person's mental and physical well-being.

Alchemists and Gold Diggers

In the Middle Ages, practitioners of alchemy, a combination of scientific exploration and mysticism, strove to understand the natural world and how to transform it. Alchemists were interested in purifying and perfecting metals and sought to change ordinary metals like lead or mercury into gold. The material that was thought to accomplish this task was known as the philosopher's stone. Of course, no such substance existed, but one alchemist, Hennig Brand, became the first person to chemically discover an element in his pursuit (read about the gross idea that led to his discovery of phosphorus on page 43).

The four elements according to the ancient Greeks

A Scientific Revolution

Building on the efforts and discoveries of the alchemists, and riding the wave of new scientific methods, pioneering chemists in the sixteenth century began to dismantle the idea of the four elements. They discovered that what had been known as "elemental" earth, for example, was made up of many components. Much of their research involved how different substances that the alchemists had isolated, such as arsenic or zinc, interacted with each other or other substances, such as gases in the air. Because some substances behaved similarly under certain circumstances, scientists began to classify them into groups in the eighteenth century, which was the beginning of the periodic table and our modern understanding of the elements.

MEET DMITRI MENDELEEV

Organizer of the Elements and Author of the Periodic Table

On February 8, 1834, in a village in Siberia, Russia, a baby boy named Dmitri Mendeleev was born. That boy would one day change the course of science forever. He came from an unusually large family. No one knows for sure, but he likely had fourteen brothers and sisters! When he was thirteen years old, his father died, and two years later the family's business burned down. In search of a better life, his mother took him from Siberia to Saint Petersburg, where he gained acceptance to college. Despite poor health, Mendeleev graduated at the top of his class, and after a short stint as a science teacher, he returned to Saint Petersburg to continue his education, focusing on chemistry.

A Wild Card

Brilliant and eccentric (he was known for his long flowing beard and uncut hair), Mendeleev poured his passion into a text called *The Principles of Chemistry*. As he worked to explain and to order the elements, he saw that atomic weight alone did not present a total picture. Inspired by the card game solitaire, he made a set of cards, one for each element known at the time, listing their chemical properties and atomic weight. Mendeleev brought these cards with him everywhere he went, shuffling and rearranging them.

Dmitri Mendeleev's set of cards was based on what scientists knew about the elements at the time. Some of the information, like the exact atomic mass numbers, was wrong, but he was still able to arrange the cards to form the periodic table we know today.

Dream Come True

As the story goes, in February 1869, Mendeleev became so obsessed with his deck of elements that he stayed awake for three days and nights arranging the cards in different orders, eventually falling into a deep sleep at his worktable. In a dream, all the elements began to dance and then snapped together into a grid. Mendeleev awoke with a vision of the periodic table. He had finally cracked the code! When elements are arranged by their atomic weight, certain properties, such as whether they are metals or gases, reappear periodically, hence the name "the periodic table of elements." In the version of the table he created, he left gaps in places where he believed unknown elements would emerge. He even predicted the likely properties of potential elements. His work has stood the test of time for more than 150 years.

HOW TO READ THE PERIODIC TABLE

The periodic table helps us make sense of the elements and their relationships to one another. Mendeleev organized the table based on the properties of each element. There is such order to the table that he predicted that some elements existed long before they were discovered.

- The periodic table is divided into ten different sections, one for each of the element categories. Each category is color coded so that you can easily distinguish each section in the grid that makes up the table.

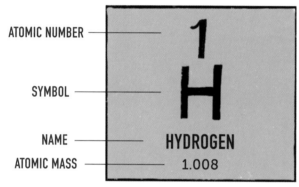

ATOMIC NUMBER —— 1

SYMBOL —— H

NAME —— HYDROGEN
ATOMIC MASS —— 1.008

- Each element has its own box. Inside each box is the name of the element and its atomic number, the element's symbol, and sometimes the atomic mass number listed below the symbol. The atomic mass number is a weighted average of all the isotopes of the element, based on how common each isotope is.

- Each element has a symbol that is made up of one or two letters. The purpose is to ensure that all scientists can easily refer to the same element even if they speak different languages. The first letter of the symbol is a capital letter, and if there is a second letter, it is lowercase.

- Each element has an atomic number. The element's atomic number is the number of protons in the nucleus of the element's atoms (see "All About Atoms" on page 10 for more detail).

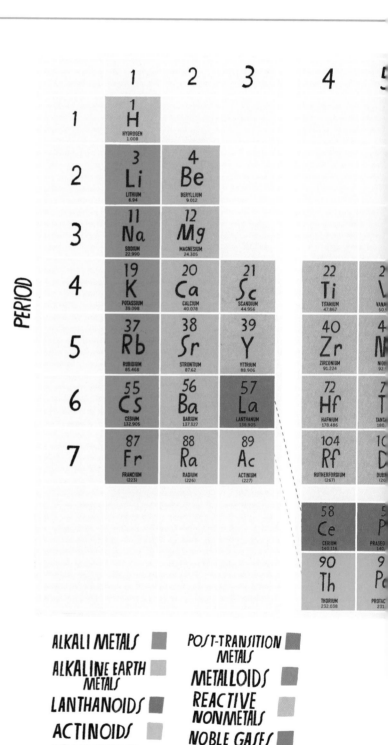

ALKALI METALS ■
ALKALINE EARTH METALS ■
LANTHANOIDS ■
ACTINOIDS ■
TRANSITION METALS ■

POST-TRANSITION METALS ■
METALLOIDS ■
REACTIVE NONMETALS ■
NOBLE GASES ■
UNKNOWN ■

GROUP

	7	8	9	10	11	12	13	14	15	16	17	18
												2 He HELIUM 4.003
							5 B BORON 10.81	6 C CARBON 12.011	7 N NITROGEN 14.007	8 O OXYGEN 15.999	9 F FLUORINE 18.998	10 Ne NEON 20.180
							13 Al ALUMINUM 26.982	14 Si SILICON 28.085	15 P PHOSPHORUS 30.974	16 S SULFUR 32.06	17 Cl CHLORINE 35.45	18 Ar ARGON 39.95
24	25 Mn MANGANESE 54.938	26 Fe IRON 55.845	27 Co COBALT 58.933	28 Ni NICKEL 58.693	29 Cu COPPER 63.546	30 Zn ZINC 65.38	31 Ga GALLIUM 69.723	32 Ge GERMANIUM 72.630	33 As ARSENIC 74.922	34 Se SELENIUM 78.971	35 Br BROMINE 79.904	36 Kr KRYPTON 83.798
42	43 Tc TECHNETIUM (97)	44 Ru RUTHENIUM 101.07	45 Rh RHODIUM 102.905	46 Pd PALLADIUM 106.42	47 Ag SILVER 107.868	48 Cd CADMIUM 112.414	49 In INDIUM 114.818	50 Sn TIN 118.710	51 Sb ANTIMONY 121.760	52 Te TELLURIUM 127.60	53 I IODINE 126.904	54 Xe XENON 131.293
74	75 Re RHENIUM 186.207	76 Os OSMIUM 190.23	77 Ir IRIDIUM 192.217	78 Pt PLATINUM 195.084	79 Au GOLD 196.967	80 Hg MERCURY 200.592	81 Tl THALLIUM 204.38	82 Pb LEAD 207.2	83 Bi BISMUTH 208.980	84 Po POLONIUM (209)	85 At ASTATINE (210)	86 Rn RADON (222)
106	107 Bh BOHRIUM (270)	108 Hs HASSIUM (269)	109 Mt MEITNERIUM (278)	110 Ds DARMSTADTIUM (281)	111 Rg ROENTGENIUM (282)	112 Cn COPERNICIUM (285)	113 Nh NIHONIUM (286)	114 Fl FLEROVIUM (289)	115 Mc MOSCOVIUM (289)	116 Lv LIVERMORIUM (293)	117 Ts TENNESSINE (294)	118 Og OGANESSON (294)
60	61 Pm PROMETHIUM (145)	62 Sm SAMARIUM 150.36	63 Eu EUROPIUM 151.964	64 Gd GADOLINIUM 157.25	65 Tb TERBIUM 158.925	66 Dy DYSPROSIUM 162.500	67 Ho HOLMIUM 164.930	68 Er ERBIUM 167.259	69 Tm THULIUM 168.934	70 Yb YTTERBIUM 173.045	71 Lu LUTETIUM 174.967	
92	93 Np NEPTUNIUM (237)	94 Pu PLUTONIUM (244)	95 Am AMERICIUM (243)	96 Cm CURIUM (247)	97 Bk BERKELIUM (247)	98 Cf CALIFORNIUM (251)	99 Es EINSTEINIUM (252)	100 Fm FERMIUM (257)	101 Md MENDELEVIUM (258)	102 No NOBELIUM (259)	103 Lr LAWRENCIUM (266)	

Periods

The rows of the periodic table are called periods. These elements have the same number of electron shells in their atoms. Periods run from left to right on the table. Elements in the first row or period have one electron shell, and those in period two have two electron shells, and so on.

Groups

The columns on a periodic table are called groups. Groups run from top to bottom on the periodic table. The elements in each group in a vertical column have the same number of electrons in their outermost shell. Elements in the same group also tend to have similar chemical properties to one another.

You might see other versions of the periodic table that group the elements using different category names, colors, and criteria. They're valid, too!

THE ELEMENT CATEGORIES

Elements are divided into categories represented by color. The placement of elements and the periods and columns of the periodic table are always the same, but if you start looking at different periodic tables, you will see that the blocks of color vary. This is because different scientists group elements together in different ways. In the periodic table in this book, the elements are divided into ten groups (with one element that stands on its own) based on their common properties.

PARTY OF ONE Hydrogen is the first element. It has one electron moving around a nucleus consisting of a single proton. It is different from all the other elements in the table, and it is not included in any of the categories.

The other elements are divided into ten different categories.

ALKALI METALS make up the first column of the periodic table. They are all reactive, meaning they have a tendency to interact and release energy when encountering other elements. Alkali metals are the most reactive of all the metals. In fact, some can cause huge explosions if placed in water or exposed to air. These vigorous reactions always produce compounds called alkalis. Alkalis are substances that measure above 7 on the pH scale (*pH* stands for "potential of hydrogen"). On the pH scale, water is neutral and measures at 7, and anything measuring above is an alkali and anything measuring below is an acid. The alkali metals are all solid at room temperature, very soft, and not dense. Some of them even float on water.

ALKALINE EARTH METALS in their pure form are shiny and silvery. However, they rarely occur in their pure form in nature, since they are, like alkali metals, reactive. We find them as compounds inside common minerals in the Earth's crust. Minerals are naturally occurring (not human-made) solids that have a definite chemical composition (a mineral will always have the same combination and number of atoms that repeat themselves in the same pattern every time). Alkaline earth metals get their name because they produce alkalis when they react with water, although they are not as reactive as the alkali metals. They are firmer and denser than the alkali metals, are solids at room temperature, and have high melting points.

LANTHANOIDS are named after lanthanum, the first element in this category. They are sometimes called rare earth metals, because they are often found mixed together in complex minerals in the Earth's crust, and when they were first discovered, they were thought to be rare. But they are actually quite abundant! These metals fit between the alkaline earth metals and the transition metals on the table, but are normally shown underneath the main table to save space. Atoms of every element in this category have two valence electrons.

ACTINOIDS also find their namesake in the first element of the category, actinium. All the elements in the actinoids category have two electrons in their outer shell. Their atoms all have seven electron shells. All the elements in this category are radioactive, and nine of the fifteen actinoids are artificially produced in laboratories. Actinoids that occur in nature are dense and have high melting points. Scientists don't know much about the physical properties of the artificial actinoids.

TRANSITION METALS hold the distinction of being the largest category on the periodic table, taking up all or part of nine columns of the table, and include thirty-one elements. In their pure state, the transition metals tend to have a shiny, metallic appearance and high melting and boiling points, with the exception of mercury.

POST-TRANSITION METALS are solid at room temperature. Like most metals, they are ductile (they can be drawn out into a thin wire without losing their toughness) and good conductors of electricity and heat. Compared to transition metals, post-transition metals are softer and have lower melting and boiling points than other metals.

METALLOIDS have both metallic and nonmetallic properties, which make them harder to classify. Metalloids usually have a metallic appearance and are solid, but they are brittle and mediocre conductors of electricity.

REACTIVE NONMETALS have a wide range of chemical properties. They are generally poor conductors of heat and electricity. This is the only category on the table to contain elements of all three states at room temperature: solid, liquid, and gas.

NOBLE GASES are the category to the far right of the periodic table. Early scientists referred to them as *noble* because they do not react with other "common" elements, like oxygen. All the members of this category are colorless gases that vary in density. Density is how compact something is: a box of feathers will weigh much less than the same size box of rocks, because the feathers are less dense than the rocks. For example, radon is fifty-four times denser than helium.

The remainder of the elements comprises a category of UNKNOWN properties, sometimes called *transactinides* to mean any element beyond the actinoids category. These elements can only be manufactured in a laboratory, and the quantities produced thus far are too small for scientists to figure out their chemical properties and assign them to a category.

▲ ▲ ▲ ▲ ▲ ▲ ▲ ▲

1 H HYDROGEN

Hydrogen holds the honor of being the first element on the periodic table, and that is because it has the simplest formula: each atom of hydrogen contains one proton and one electron. Hydrogen is also number one in the universe, comprising 75 percent of all atoms. A significant amount of hydrogen can be found in the sun and stars. The sun alone consumes 600 million tons (over 544 million tonnes) of hydrogen per second, and this constant burning of hydrogen gives off the heat and light that sustains life on Earth.

Category: None
Year discovered: 1766
Discovered by: Henry Cavendish, a British scientist

▲ ▲

The Buddy System

Hydrogen loves to buddy up, bonding with itself or other elements. Combined with oxygen, hydrogen forms the water that fills our seas, rivers, lakes, and clouds. A different combination of hydrogen and oxygen produces hydrogen peroxide, which is used to clean and sterilize. The white sugar you use to make cookies is hydrogen combined with carbon and oxygen. Large planets such as Jupiter are vast balls of hydrogen mixed with other gases, like helium and methane.

Powers Put to Good Use

The power of hydrogen is vast and able to be stored in fuel cells. A fuel cell is a device that creates usable electricity through a chemical reaction of positively charged hydrogen ions with oxygen or another element. They are a bit like batteries. Small fuel cells could be a way to power laptop computers and cell phones. Large fuel cells can power buses, cars, or entire buildings.

2 He HELIUM

Helium is named for the Greek god of the sun, Helios, because scientists first viewed helium as an unexplained line surrounding the sun during a solar eclipse. Chemists in the mid–1800s, when helium was first observed, had yet to discover the element in the lab, because it is a noble gas. Noble gases don't react with or commonly bond with other elements, making them hard to detect in typical experiments; noble gases prefer to sit twiddling their thumbs while the other elements react with each other. Helium gas was eventually discovered emitting from heated ore (ore is a rock or mineral that contains metal) on Earth. Today helium is extracted from natural gas that comes out of the ground.

▲ ▲

Up, Up, and Away

Helium is the second-lightest element after hydrogen. It is so light that it tends to escape the Earth's atmosphere into space. While a quarter of all atoms in the universe are helium, it is pretty rare on Earth. Helium is lighter than air and, like other noble gases, is inert, so it won't react to other chemicals and won't catch fire, making it useful to fill hot-air balloons, blimps, and, famously, party balloons.

Category: Noble gas
Year discovered: 1895
Discovered by: Sir William Ramsay, a Scottish chemist, and independently by Per Teodor Cleve and Nils Abraham Langlet, Swedish chemists
Fun fact: Helium was the only element observed in space before it was found on Earth.

3 Li LITHIUM

Lithium is a soft and silvery-white metal. Of all the metals, it is the lightest—it can float on water (although it will also react with the liquid vigorously). Lithium is highly reactive and flammable, so care must be taken in storing it, as there's a chance it could react upon contact with air or water.

▲ ▲ ▲ ▲ ▲ ▲ ▲ ▲ ▲ ▲ ▲ ▲ ▲ ▲ ▲ ▲ ▲ ▲ ▲

Category: Alkali metal
Discovered: 1817
Discovered by: Johan August Arfwedson, a Swedish chemist
Fun fact: Lithium is a metal, but it's soft enough to cut with a butter knife.

Social Butterfly

Lithium likes company. In fact, it isn't found in nature by itself, but is always bonded to other elements. You can find it bonded to chlorine, from the other side of the periodic table, in lithium chloride, which is used to dry out the air in humid environments. Lithium is usually found in salt compounds; the ocean is estimated to contain more than 200 billion tons of lithium as salt.

Powers Put to Good Use

Lithium's reactivity makes it a great conductor of heat and electricity. One of its common uses is the lithium battery. Lithium batteries contain enormous power and are ideal for running small watches, laptops, and cameras. Lithium carbonate is used to treat bipolar disorder and helps even out the severe mood swings caused by this mental illness. Lithium is used in the construction of airplanes. Combined with aluminum, it forms an alloy that is lightweight but strong, making planes that are lighter and use less fuel.

4 Be BERYLLIUM

Although it is a light and stiff metal, you won't find beryllium in many everyday items, because it is rare and toxic to humans. Only a supernova (the cosmic explosion at the end of a supergiant star's lifetime) can generate beryllium, making it uncommon.

▲ ▲

Light as a Feather, Stiff as a Board

Because of its low density and atomic weight, beryllium is almost transparent to X-rays, and it is often used for X-ray tubes. Combined with copper, it forms a non-sparking, high-strength metal in tools that are safe to use around flammable substances. Beryllium is expensive, but its strength, lightness, high melting point, and resistance to corrosion make it ideal for spacecraft—beryllium mirrors were used in the James Webb Space Telescope, the successor to the Hubble Space Telescope.

Category: Alkaline earth metal
Year discovered: 1797
Discovered by: Nicolas-Louis Vauquelin, a French chemist
Fun fact: Beryllium was originally called *glucinium* from the Greek word for sweet, since its salts taste sweet. Humans quickly discovered that beryllium is also toxic and should *never* be tasted, and the name was later changed.

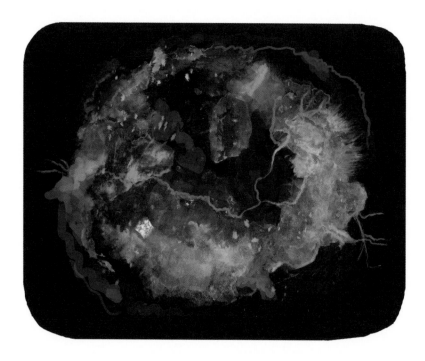

Beryllium is the product of a supernova.

5 B BORON

While its name implies it is a bit of a snore, boron is a secret agent in the periodic table. Boron compounds are some of the toughest stuff on Earth. Pure boron isn't found naturally in our environment, but is part of mineral compounds.

▲ ▲

The Buddy System

Boron isn't a bore when it combines with other elements. Introduce it to nitrogen and you will get boron nitride crystals that are nearly as hard as diamonds. Boron carbide is one of the hardest known substances and is used in the armor of military tanks.

Around the House

There is a good likelihood that a boron compound is part of your everyday life. The obvious occurrence is in borax, the salts of boric acid, which is the foundation for many laundry detergents and household cleaners. Our secret agent boron strengthens heat-resistant glassware, like liquid measuring cups and Pyrex brand baking dishes.

Category: Metalloid
Year discovered: 1808
Discovered by: Louis-Josef Gay-Lussac and Louis-Jacques Thénard, French chemists, and Sir Humphry Davy, a British chemist
Fun fact: The squishy, tactile "slime" popular in online videos is made from boron in the form of borax. When borax is mixed with glue, the molecules tangle, creating a substance that is neither a liquid nor a solid.

6 C CARBON

Hydrogen may be the glue that holds the universe together, but carbon is the foundation of all life. An entire field of study called organic chemistry exists to study carbon compounds. Every living thing contains some compound of carbon. Because of its ability to bond easily with other atoms, carbon forms long, resilient chains called polymers. A polymer is a large molecule made up of many smaller molecules linked in a bond, like beads on a string. Organic carbon polymers like cellulose occur naturally and are essential to all living things, forming the cell walls of plants. Produced in labs and factories, synthetic polymers include nylon fibers and plastics. Synthetic polymers are incredibly useful because of their resiliency, strength, and flexibility, but that same stability means they do not easily biodegrade in the environment and pose pollution hazards.

Category: Reactive nonmetal
Year discovered: Prehistoric
Discovered by: Unknown
Fun fact: The tattoos of Ötzi the Iceman, a 5,300-year-old corpse found frozen in the Alps, were inked from carbon (and carbon remains the primary ingredient in black tattoo ink!).

Formation Wizard

Carbon has the greatest number of allotropes of any element. Allotropes are different physical forms in which an element can exist. Arranged in stacked sheets, carbon atoms form soft, pliable graphite. Arranged in an interlocking lattice, they form one of the hardest materials in the world: the diamond. Rolled into cylinders or spheres, carbon forms fullerene, a substance that is up to one hundred times stronger than steel.

All-Encompassing

Carbon is found in nearly everything we touch, from food to shelter to clothing. Steel, gunpowder, pencils, motors, filtration systems, lubricants, fuel, and ink all have carbon as their foundation. It is the basis for the manufacturing marvel graphene, a material that's stronger than steel and more flexible than rubber.

Climate Change Instigator

Carbon has a dark side. When fossil fuels like coal and oil are burned, they are converted to carbon dioxide. And when an excess of carbon dioxide enters the atmosphere, it traps heat from the sun, warming the Earth in a process known as global warming.

ALLOTROPES OF CARBON

GRAPHITE

DIAMOND

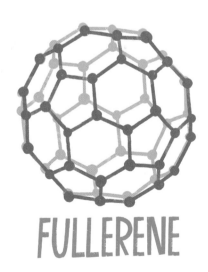

FULLERENE

NITROGEN

Nitrogen makes up 78 percent of our atmosphere! Early in our planet's history, built-up nitrogen in the Earth's crust was released into our atmosphere in volcanic eruptions. As a gas, nitrogen is colorless, odorless, and considered inert, which means it is not typically reactive. In its liquid form, nitrogen is colorless and odorless and looks similar to water.

Category: Reactive nonmetal
Year discovered: 1772
Discovered by: Daniel Rutherford, a Scottish chemist
Fun fact: Titan, Saturn's largest moon, has an almost entirely nitrogen atmosphere. It is the only moon in the solar system to have a dense atmosphere.

Does a Body Good

Nitrogen's abundance is fortunate: it is essential to life on Earth. Although the human body is only 3 percent nitrogen, it is still the fourth most abundant element in your body. We find nitrogen in nearly all organic matter. Plants rely on nitrogen for nutrients, and they do the job of being "nitrogen fixers," trapping it in more usable forms for other organisms to use. Even though we are surrounded by nitrogen-rich air, we rely on those plants in our diet to get enough nitrogen.

The Buddy System

Nitrogen forms a strong bond with itself in the form of N_2, which is in the air all around us. An important nitrogen compound is colorless ammonia gas, which is liquefied into a fertilizer for crops. About 80 percent of the ammonia created by humans is used as fertilizer. The other 20 percent is used in plastics, textiles, pesticides, dyes, and cleaning solutions.

THE NITROGEN CYCLE

1 Nitrogen in the atmosphere is converted to nitrates by lightning and brought to the soil by rain.

2 Plants absorb nitrates through their roots and use them to build proteins and grow.

3 Nitrogen in the soil is converted into nitrates by bacteria and nodules in plant roots.

4 Animals eat the plants and absorb the nitrates by converting them into animal proteins.

5 Nitrogen returns to the soil through animal droppings (poop and pee) as well as decomposing animal carcasses.

8 O OXYGEN

Oxygen is the most abundant element on Earth and the third most common in the universe, after hydrogen and helium. That abundance of oxygen, along with its wide-reaching reactivity, makes it crucial for our everyday lives. Oxygen sustains us in the air we breathe and is the foundation of humankind. High levels of atmospheric oxygen are what enabled multicellular organisms and eventually more advanced life forms, such as humans, to develop and evolve.

▲ ▲

Category: Reactive nonmetal
Year discovered: 1774
Discovered by: Joseph Priestley, a British clergyman and amateur chemist, and independently by Carl Wilhelm Scheele, a Swedish chemist
Fun fact: If we someday discover another planet with an oxygen-rich atmosphere, we will know that extraterrestrial life exists, since only living things release oxygen.

The Cycle of Life

When animals need energy, they take in oxygen through respiration. (They can't burn sugars without it.) The oxygen returns to the atmosphere in the form of carbon dioxide. In turn, plants combine the carbon dioxide with water and convert the two back into oxygen and sugars through a process called photosynthesis. This oxygen–carbon dioxide cycle sustains life on Earth.

The Buddy System

Oxygen wants to interact with all the elements (those snobby noble gases still ignore it, though!), often in combustible ways. When things combust, producing light and heat (a flame), it is usually because they are reacting with oxygen. For example, a candle flame is created through the interaction of the carbon in the wax and oxygen in the air, but if you place a glass over the flame and remove the source of oxygen, the flame will go out.

Powers Put to Good Use

We use oxygen to power our bodies by releasing energy stored in cells every time we breathe, but we also harness the power of oxygen to fuel much of our world. Car engines are powered by the combustion of gasoline and oxygen. Oxygen is stored in tanks when we explore oxygen-poor environments, like underwater scuba diving, high-altitude mountain climbing, or outer space, where we need oxygen not only to breathe, but also in order for rocket fuel to burn.

A candle flame burns because the carbon in the wax interacts in a combustible way with the oxygen in the air. If you place a glass over the candle, isolating it from the oxygen in the air, the flame will go out.

FLUORINE

Fluorine is considered the most reactive element on the periodic table. In its pure form, it is a toxic yellowish gas so reactive that a tiny amount in the air can kill a human being. Hydrofluoric acid can burn through hard substances like steel, glass, and brick. Its toxicity made the process of isolating it incredibly difficult. It was not until 1886 that Henri Moissan isolated fluorine, later earning him a Nobel Prize in 1906.

Category: Reactive nonmetal

Year discovered: 1886

Discovered by: Henry Moissan, a French chemist

Fun fact: The term *fluorescent* comes from the fluorine-rich mineral fluorite, which glows when exposed to light.

▲ ▲

From Toxic Gas to Healthy Smiles

In small amounts and combined with other elements, fluorine transforms from deadly gas to helpful ally. In fact, it is considered essential for humans. The fluoride in your toothpaste is made from fluorine combined with sodium, and it protects our teeth from decay. Much of the tap water in the United States has fluoride added, because scientists in the 1940s discovered that people who lived in areas with high fluoride levels in their water had fewer cavities.

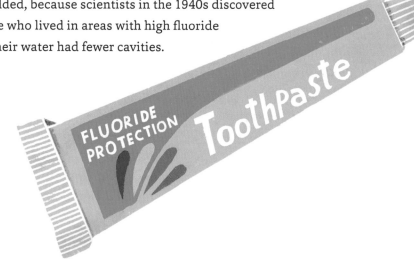

10 Ne NEON

Neon is an extremely rare element. It makes up 0.0018 percent of the Earth's atmosphere. As the opposite of its neighbor fluorine, it is the least reactive of all the elements. It refuses to interact with any other element—even fluorine. In its natural state, it is a colorless gas, but when you cool it below -411° Fahrenheit (-246° Celsius), it turns to liquid.

Category: Noble gas
Year discovered: 1898
Discovered by: Sir William Ramsay and Morris Travers, British chemists
Fun fact: Liquefied neon is sometimes used in cryonics: the practice of freezing bodies quickly after death in the hope that they might be revived in the future.

Under the Neon Lights

French engineer Georges Claude first produced neon tube lights in 1910. Homeowners weren't interested in the lights because of their orange glow, so Claude bent them into letter shapes, sold them to shop owners for signage, and the original neon sign was born. When high-voltage electricity runs through a tube filled with neon, the gas glows a bright orange red. Today, all brightly colored illuminated signs are called neon, but only *orange* neon lights contain actual neon. Other colors of "neon" lights are made from mercury vapor or krypton tubes coated in phosphor.

11 Na SODIUM

You probably know sodium as table salt, but did you know that what you add to your food isn't pure sodium, but actually sodium chloride? Sodium is extremely reactive and it never occurs in a pure state in nature. It is always formed into compounds. In its pure form, sodium is silvery white and soft enough to cut with a knife. It has to be stored in special containers that protect it from reacting to air and water.

Category: Alkali metal
Year discovered: 1807
Discovered by: Sir Humphry Davy, a British chemist
Fun fact: In ancient Egypt, sodium mixtures were used to preserve dead bodies as mummies.

▲▲▲ ▲ ▲▲▲ ▲ ▲ ▲▲▲ ▲ ▲ ▲▲▲ ▲ ▲ ▲▲▲ ▲ ▲ ▲▲▲ ▲

More Than Table Salt

Sodium compounds do more than make your French fries tasty. Sodium hydroxide is used in body soap and in lye, which we use to unclog drains. Sodium bicarbonate is in some carbonated beverages and is the main ingredient of dry-chemical fire extinguishers. Sodium sulfate is used to make paper and glass. Sodium chloride, which is also called halite, comprises 80 percent of the dissolved contents of ocean and seawater.

Does a Body Good

Sodium is an important element in your body, too. It absorbs and transports nutrients in your system, maintains your blood pressure and fluid balance, transmits your nerve signals, and contracts and relaxes your muscles—just to name a few functions!

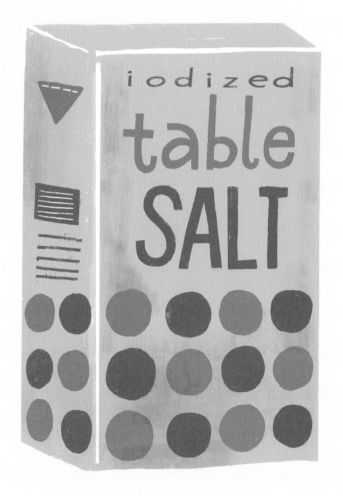

12 Mg MAGNESIUM

Magnesium is an extrovert element that, out in the world, you will find only in combination with other elements, such as carbon, calcium, and oxygen. Since much of the magnesium on Earth is in the Earth's mantle (the layer between the crust and the core), it is extracted primarily from seawater, but it is also found in rock ores.

▲ ▲

Category: Alkaline earth metal
Year discovered: 1755
Discovered by: Joseph Black, a British scientist
Fun fact: Every cubic mile of ocean or seawater contains approximately 12 billion pounds (5.44 billion kilograms) of magnesium.

In a Flash

When small amounts of magnesium are ground into powder, it becomes super flammable. The bright white light it creates when ignited makes magnesium powder useful in pyrotechnics and flares, but it burns at one of the highest temperatures of any material—4,000° Fahrenheit (2,200° Celsius)—resulting in a flame too hot to be extinguished with water.

Green Thumb

Magnesium is needed for almost all living organisms and plays a role in photosynthesis. Plants absorb magnesium from the soil. That magnesium is the central atom of chlorophyll, the green pigment that allows plants to use light to convert carbon dioxide and water into glucose and oxygen.

Does a Body Good

Human bodies also need magnesium. We get it from eating plants and the animals that eat plants. Up to 60 percent of our bodies' magnesium maintains our bone structure. The remainder helps us with more than three hundred biochemical reactions, including nerve, muscle, and heart functions, the regulation of blood sugar levels, and the release of energy from food.

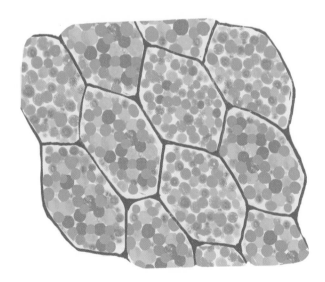

Magnesium is the central atom in the chlorophyll molecules in plant cells.

PARIS EXPOSITION 1855

13 Al ALUMINUM

When people hear the word *aluminum,* they think about the foil we use to wrap our food. But soft and malleable aluminum is one of the most-used metals in the world. It has a vast range of applications beyond the kitchen. It is so common today that it is surprising to learn that scientists did not discover it until the early 1800s. And it took a few more years after that to work out how to extract it from it is main source, the ores of the mineral bauxite.

Category: Post-transition metal
Year discovered: 1825
Discovered by: Hans Christian Ørsted, a Danish chemist
Fun fact: The aluminum used in the outer shell of airplanes protects them from lightning strikes. The aluminum conducts electrical currents from the lightning to pass along the fuselage of the plane and exit through the tail or wing without affecting the interior of the cabin.

Regal History

At one time, aluminum was considered more valuable than gold. It was so expensive to mine that it was considered to be for the rich and privileged. It is rumored that at the court of Napoleon III of France, visiting heads of state would be served delicacies on aluminum plates to denote their superiority, while dukes of lesser status were served on gold. An aluminum bar lay beside the Crown Jewels of France at the 1855 Paris Exposition.

Recycling Queen

Because it is useful but expensive and difficult to mine, aluminum is widely recycled. The process of recycling aluminum uses just 5 percent of the energy needed to mine aluminum. Fortunately, soda cans, of which billions are produced each year, are almost 100 percent pure aluminum and can be recycled easily and cheaply.

Powers Put to Good Use

Aluminum is lightweight and resistant to corrosion. These properties make it ideal as window frames, food containers, aircraft fuselage, and the casing around modern touch screens. It is an excellent conductor of electricity, and it is combined with other metals in electrical cables.

THE TEN MOST ABUNDANT ELEMENTS IN EARTH'S CRUST

Earth's iron is found mostly in the core and the mantle, not the crust. The inner and outer cores are believed to be made up of an alloy of iron–nickel that makes up an estimated 35 percent of Earth's entire mass.

Oxygen is the most abundant element in Earth's crust. While we think of oxygen as a gas that we breathe in our atmosphere, it is also one of the primary components of the minerals that make up the majority of the crust.

More than 90 percent of Earth's crust is composed of silicate minerals, which contain the elements silicon and oxygen in some proportion, making silicon the second most abundant element in Earth's crust.

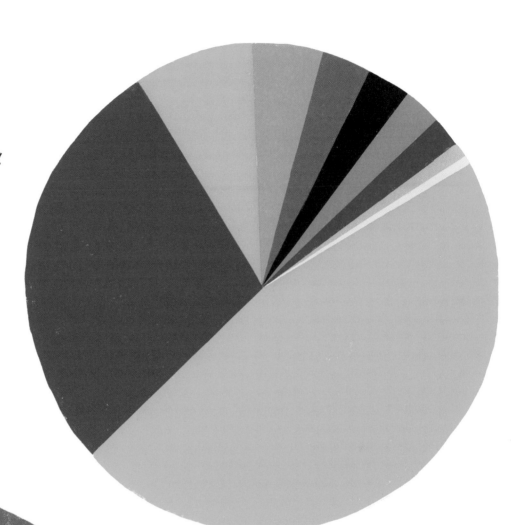

OXYGEN 46.10%
SILICON 28.20%
ALUMINUM 8.23%
IRON 5.63%
CALCIUM 4.15%
SODIUM 2.36%
MAGNESIUM 2.33%
POTASSIUM 2.09%
TITANIUM .565%
HYDROGEN .14%

EARTH'S CRUST

MANTLE

OUTER CORE

INNER CORE

14 Si SILICON

Silicon is the second most common element on Earth next to oxygen, which is also its biggest ally. Approximately 95 percent of the minerals that comprise Earth's rocks contain silicon, and almost all of those rocks are compounds of silicon and oxygen, known as silicates. One common silicate is the naturally occurring sand that lines the beaches of the world.

Category: Metalloid
Year discovered: 1824
Discovered by: Jöns Jacob Berzelius, a Swedish chemist
Fun fact: Humans have long found silicon useful. Many Stone Age tools, like arrowheads and cutting implements, were made from silica-based rock, such as quartz and flint.

▲ ▲

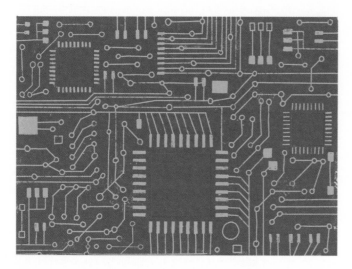

Computer motherboards are covered in integrated circuits made from silicon.

Crystal Clear

Silicon has become one of the most important elements in the past fifty years because of its fundamental role in computers. An entire region of California is named Silicon Valley because so many computer companies are based in the area. Microchips regulate the flow of electricity with the help of silicon. On its own, silicon is a poor conductor of electricity, but when small quantities of other elements are added to silicon, it becomes a more useful semiconductor, conducting current in a unique way.

Powers Put to Good Use

This versatile element is also used to turn sunlight into electricity in solar panels. Glass, bricks, and ceramic clay are made from silicates. Silicon is used to make silicones, which are used as household sealants, industrial lubricants, and flexible cooking tools.

15 P PHOSPHORUS

Phosphorus has three main forms: the poisonous and deadly white phosphorus, which ignites in the air; the safer and more stable red phosphorus; and the rarely seen black phosphorus. Although it plays a part in the maintenance of all living things, phosphorus is never found in its pure state in our natural world.

Category: Reactive nonmetal
Year discovered: 1669
Discovered by: Hennig Brand, a German merchant and alchemist
Fun fact: The strip on the outside of a box of matches contains phosphorus, which ignites when the head of the match strikes it.

▲ ▲

The "Pee" Story

The German alchemist Hennig Brand first discovered phosphorus in the seventeenth century. In an all-consuming quest for the mythical philosopher's stone, Brand decided to boil urine (maybe it was the golden color that gave him the idea?). The result was an eerie glowing substance: white phosphorus reacting with the oxygen. Brand was pleased with his discovery, and, convinced of the substance's magical powers, he kept it a guarded secret for years. Later the element was given the name *phosphorus*, meaning "giver of light."

In Our DNA

Phosphates are created from the bond of phosphorus and oxygen. Phosphates are important to all living things, as they are part of the framework of our DNA and a component of ATP (adenosine triphosphate), which is how our body stores energy in our cells. Even our bones are made of hardened calcium phosphate.

Growing Pains

Phosphorus is an ingredient in fertilizers, which help plant crops grow. However, when phosphates enter the water supply from overuse or pollution, they can cause overgrowth of algae and other plants, tainting water supplies.

PEE-YEW! YOU STINK!

Pure **sulfur** has no smell, but many of its compounds are real stinkers! Sulfur compounds called thiols are responsible for the pungent aroma of skunk spray, rotten eggs, and the gas you pass. That farty smell is a gas your body creates when it breaks down foods with sulfur in them.

Sitting below sulfur on the periodic table, **selenium** smells as bad as its neighbor. Many chemists claim that what emits from hydrogen selenide is the worst smell in the world (other chemists decided to take their word for it).

You might have smelled **bromine**'s distinctive sharp odor at a pool or hot tub where it disinfects the water. The element is named after the Greek word for stench, *bromos*.

Closely related to sulfur and selenium, **tellurium** can also clear a room. Just half a microgram of tellurium absorbed into the body can give a person extreme garlic breath for thirty hours.

English chemist Smithson Tennant was so put off by the pungent smell of **osmium** that he named it after the Greek word for odor, *osme*.

16 SULFUR

Famous for its scent, sulfur is one of the few elements that can be found in its pure form in nature. This yellow, crystalline element can be found mainly in volcanic craters and hot springs.

▲ ▲

Powers Put to Good Use

About 85 percent of sulfur is converted to sulfuric acid, a corrosive, oily liquid that is an ingredient in fertilizer, oil refining, and the removal of rust from iron and steel. Sulfur's compounds harden natural rubber to use in tires, preserve dried fruit, and make battery acids. The element also has antibacterial properties and is used in medicines.

Category: Reactive nonmetal

Year discovered: Known since prehistoric times, recognized as an element in 1777

Discovered by: Antoine-Laurent Lavoisier, a French chemist

Fun fact: Sulfur dioxide was used to fumigate homes from pests beginning in ancient times, a practice that continued into the nineteenth century.

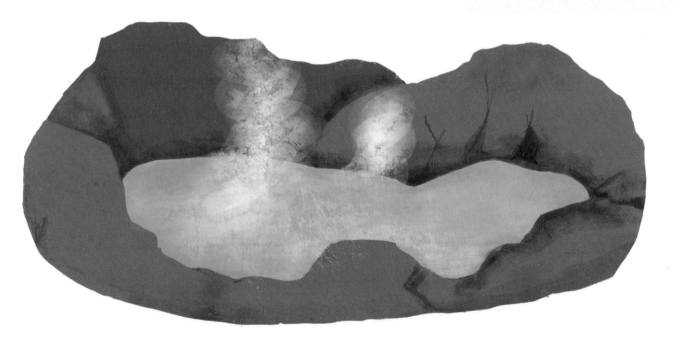

Deep beneath the surface, water heats up due to increasing pressure and proximity to the Earth's core, dissolving the sulfur in the surrounding soil and rocks. The sulfur binds with oxygen to form the compound sulfate, which gives hot springs their stinky smell.

17 Cl CHLORINE

In its pure form, which is never found in nature, chlorine is a greenish-yellow gas that is highly reactive and dangerous. But mixed with other elements, chlorine is useful and necessary for bodily functions. It is used by muscles and nerves and is present in our perspiration. Our stomachs create hydrochloric acid to help digest the food we eat.

▲ ▲

The Buddy System

Chlorine forms a number of compounds, and many of them are quite useful to us. Sodium chloride, also known as table salt, is used to season food. Hydrogen chloride, when mixed with water, forms hydrochloric acid, a strong commercial acid used to clean rust from steel.

Powers Put to Good Use

Chlorine is found in paper products, dyes, textiles, medicines, antiseptics, insecticides, solvents, paints, batteries, gelatin, and PVC, a very tough plastic material. It is famous for its role in keeping swimming pools free of germs.

Risky Business

In its natural gas form, chlorine can be harmful to human health. Chlorine irritates the respiratory system, and inhaling it may cause pulmonary edema, a buildup of fluid in the lungs that can lead to difficulty in breathing. Sadly, for this reason, it has been used as a chemical weapon.

Category: Reactive nonmetal

Year discovered: 1774

Discovered by: Carl Wilhelm Scheele, a Swedish chemist

Fun fact: Chlorine is a common additive to drinking water in the developed world today, a practice that began in response to a typhoid outbreak in England in 1897. Chlorine brought the epidemic under control by killing the bacteria in the water supply that was causing the disease.

SWIMMING POOL

chlorine tablets

Solvent

500 ml

House
and
Garden
INSECT SPRAY

KILLS INSECTS

BLEACH
SCRUB

NET WT 14 OZ

18 Ar ARGON

Argon has a reputation as the lazy element, the couch potato of the periodic table. Named after the Greek word *argos*, meaning "idle" or "inactive," argon, like the other noble gases, is uninterested in combining with other elements. It is, however, the third most abundant gas in the Earth's atmosphere after nitrogen and oxygen.

Category: Noble gas
Year discovered: 1894
Discovered by: Lord Rayleigh and Sir William Ramsay, British chemists
Fun fact: Argon is colorless and inert, but if you charge it with an electric current, it emits the purple-blue glow we use in illuminated signs.

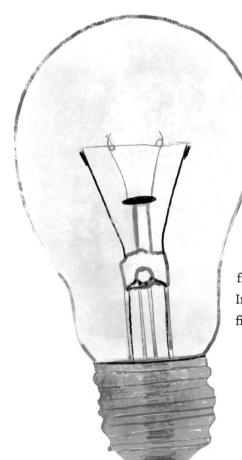

Powers Put to Good Use

Argon may be "lazy," but its inertness is what makes it useful. Because it is abundant in the air, argon is inexpensive to obtain: air is first cooled into a liquid, and then the individual gases are extracted based on their boiling points. In activities that require high temperatures, such as welding, argon gas surrounds the flame, preventing the metals from reacting with oxygen (a not-so-lazy gas that wants to react with *everything*). Argon also doesn't conduct heat well, so it is helpful in insulating from outside temperatures; you will find it between windowpanes. Incandescent light bulbs are filled with argon, which allows the filament to burn hot and bright without reacting with oxygen.

19 K POTASSIUM

Potassium, a soft, waxy metal you can cut with a knife, is highly reactive and never found in its pure form in nature. However, as a compound, it is a useful element. In fact, we could not live without it.

▲ ▲

Potash-ium

If you burn plants and dissolve the remaining ash into water, you will find yourself with a solution of almost entirely potassium salts. This substance is called potash, and it has been used as a soil fertilizer for centuries, improving soil nutrition and plant growth. Among its many benefits to plants, potassium plays a major role in the regulation of water, improves drought resistance, and activates enzymes that help plants grow.

Does a Body Good

Potassium is a necessary nutrient for life. It is an electrolyte, which carries electrical impulses across cells. Along with sodium, it is crucial for proper muscle contraction. When you sweat or have a stomach bug, you lose electrolytes and your potassium levels decrease. Potassium deficiency can cause weakness, cramps, and even mental confusion. When this happens, electrolytes need to be replaced to keep bodily fluids healthy. Bananas, apricots, lentils, broccoli, and cantaloupe provide good amounts of potassium to our bodies.

Category: Alkali metal
Year discovered: 1807
Discovered by: Sir Humphry Davy, a British chemist
Fun fact: Bananas, because they contain a high amount of potassium, are radioactive! In truth, everything we eat is somewhat radioactive.

# CALCIUM

Calcium is all around us in the Earth's crust. Calcium is also *in* us. You have around 2 pounds (910 grams) of calcium in your bones and teeth. In its pure form, calcium is a silvery metal, but it is never found in nature, because it reacts with both air and water. The primary calcium compound we find in nature is calcium carbonate in limestone rock, sea coral, and seashells.

▲ ▲

Category: Alkaline earth metal
Year discovered: 1808
Discovered by: Sir Humphry Davy, a British chemist
Fun fact: Calcium is the reason our bones show up in X-rays. The calcium in our bones absorbs the radiation from the rays, while the soft tissue lets the rays pass through. The result: our bones show up white on the film!

Does a Body Good

You have probably heard the ad campaigns letting you know that milk "does a body good," but it is the calcium in the milk that leads to strong bones. Milk is biologically designed for mothers to give their young the essential vitamins and minerals they need to grow. Because calcium is essential to our bodies' function, it is stored in our bones and teeth as calcium phosphate. If we don't have calcium in our diet, our body will pull calcium from our bones, making them brittle or causing them to not develop properly. Foods rich in calcium include dairy products, dark green leafy vegetables, beans, and some types of fish.

Chalk It Up to Calcium

Calcium carbonate, the main component of limestone, is a chalky, sedimentary rock made up of deposits of coral and seashells. Limestone is used decoratively in polished tiles and countertops, but it is also an important component of concrete. Another chalky substance that contains calcium is calcium sulfate, known as gypsum, used in building construction. Gypsum is also employed to make the casts that protect healing broken bones (calcium on calcium). You have probably held gypsum before. It is what chalk is made of!

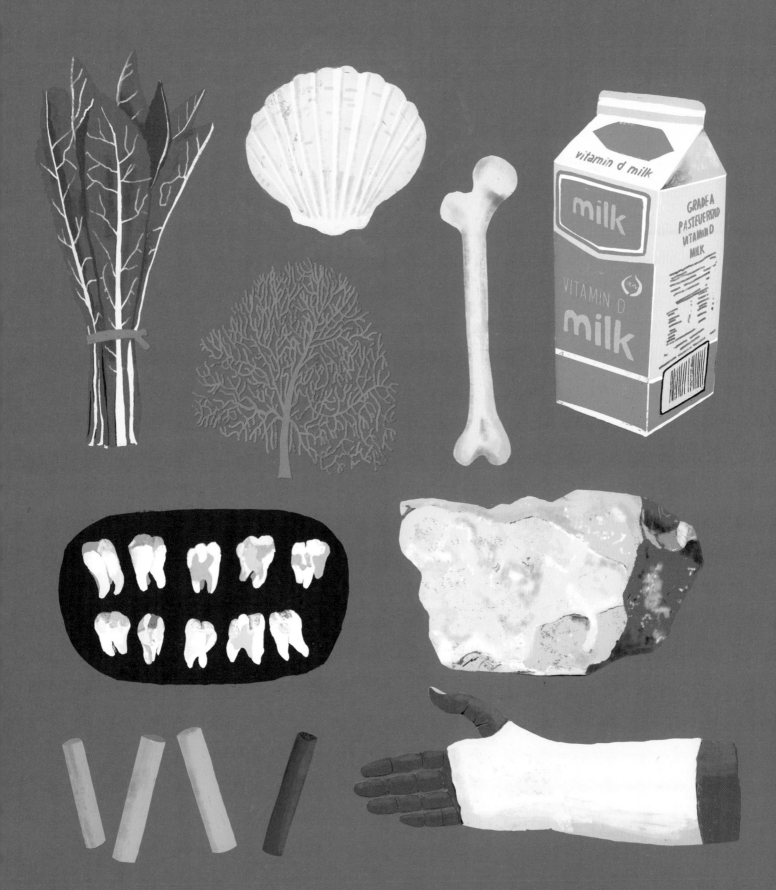

21 Sc SCANDIUM

Scandium is a soft, lightweight metal similar to aluminum that would seem to have many uses. So why have you never heard of it? Well, scandium is not so much rare in the Earth's crust as it is spread thinly throughout. Unlike more common metals, scandium is not concentrated in one place, so large volumes of material must be mined and processed to produce a tiny amount of usable ore. The total world trade of scandium is just 5 to 15 tons (4.5 to 13.6 tonnes) a year.

▲ ▲

Category: Transition metal
Year discovered: 1879
Discovered by: Lars Fredrik Nilson, a Swedish chemist
Fun fact: The father of the periodic table, Dmitri Mendeleev (page 16), predicted the existence of an element between calcium and titanium in 1871, but it took another decade for Nilson to find it. Nilson named the element after his native Sweden, part of Scandinavia.

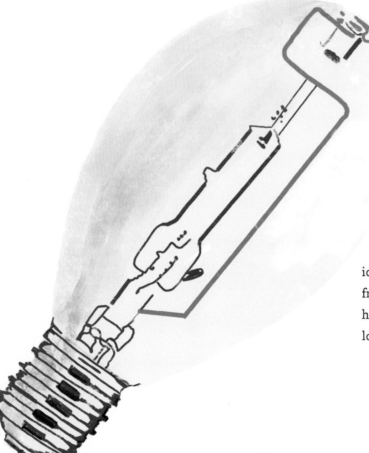

A Little Bit Goes a Long Way

Despite its limited production, scandium is put to good use. Just 0.1 percent of scandium improves the strength of aluminum alloy, creating a resilient metal ideal for aircraft and sporting equipment, like bicycle frames and baseball bats. You can find scandium in metal halide lights, the bright bluish lights favored in parking lots, big-box retail stores, and sports arenas.

ENDANGERED ELEMENTS

These elements will not disappear from Earth (with the exception of helium, which escapes into space). But human use has spread concentrations of them out across the planet. This makes them hard to recover, and thus "endangered." You may think of animals when you hear the word *endangered*, but elements are also called endangered, even though they are aren't dying or disappearing—rather, when an element is endangered, our access to it is limited.

Although it is the second most abundant element in the universe, the **helium** we have on Earth originates from the decay of natural uranium and thorium and has built up over billions of years, and we are using it more quickly than it can be created.

A component of touch screens in the form of indium tin oxide, **indium's** demand has soared in recent years. Scientists are developing more efficient ways to extract the ore from the earth and from discarded devices.

Used in modern agriculture as a fertilizer, supplies of **phosphorous** are forecast to fall below current demand in thirty years. However, scientists are working on ways to recover phosphorous from our urine in wastewater!

Green technologies, like wind turbines and hybrid cars, are dependent on rare earth elements (REEs)—the fifteen **lanthanoids**, along with **scandium** and **yttrium**. Their similar chemical properties make them challenging and expensive to isolate from one another, and demand is beginning to outpace the supply.

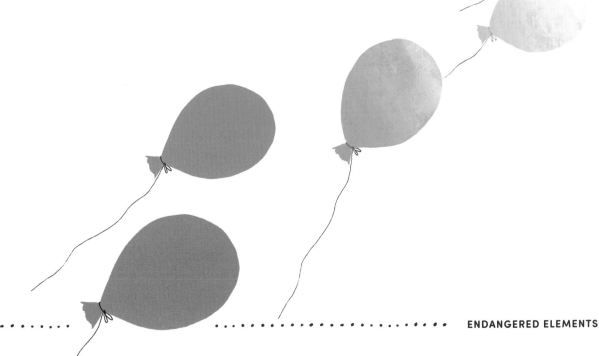

22 Ti TITANIUM

Named after the Titans of Greek mythology, titanium is one of the superheroes of the periodic table due to its strength, lightness, and resistance to corrosion. Titanium ore is plentiful on Earth, but it is difficult to extract, which makes it an expensive resource.

▲ ▲

Category: Transition metal
Year discovered: 1791
Discovered by: William Gregor, a British clergyman and mineralogist
Fun fact: Satellite images from NASA probes show that the moon is covered in clusters of titanium-rich rock. While titanium makes up about 1 percent of rocks on Earth, the lunar rocks contain up to 10 percent titanium.

Tickle Me Titanium

Titanium is found in the majority of igneous rocks (rocks formed from the cooling of lava). Pick up a handful of sand, and you are holding titanium. Pure titanium metal is extracted from titanium dioxide through the Kroll process, where titanium-rich sand is heated with carbon and chlorine gas to produce titanium tetrachloride, known as *tickle*. The liquid tickle is in turn combined with magnesium, which helps release the pure titanium metal.

Powers Put to Good Use

Despite its cost, the same strength and light weight that make titanium the choice for rockets and jet engines also makes it popular for sports equipment, like bike frames, golf clubs, and Rollerblades. It rarely causes allergies and can be worn safely on your body as jewelry, but also inside your body as artificial joints or as metal plates for repairing your skull. Titanium is not easily broken down by body fluids, and bone will grow and attach to titanium implants.

Wonder Twin Powers, Activate!

When titanium meets oxygen, titanium dioxide is created, unlocking another amazing set of uses. The substance is white and opaque and is used as the base for paint and in the paper of some books, keeping the ink from one side of the page from showing through to the other side. Titanium dioxide refracts light and absorbs ultraviolet rays, protecting your skin as an active ingredient in sunscreen.

23 V VANADIUM

Vanadium is a tough worker and a team player. When this shiny, silvery metal is alloyed with steel, the result is a stronger and lighter material. In fact, Henry Ford credited vanadium steel as essential to the first mass-produced automobile, the Model T.

▲ ▲ ▲ ▲ ▲ ▲ ▲ ▲ ▲ ▲ ▲ ▲ ▲ ▲ ▲ ▲ ▲ ▲ ▲ ▲

Category: Transition metal
Year discovered: 1801
Discovered by: Andrés Manuel del Rio, a Spanish-Mexican scientist
Fun fact: Vanadium is named after the Scandinavian goddess Vanadis, who is said to have traveled on a chariot pulled by two cats.

Powers Put to Good Use

Vanadium makes steel stronger and lighter when even 0.15 percent is added to the alloy. Because it retains its hardness at high temperatures, vanadium alloy steel is ideal for weapons and tools. Ancient metalworkers used vanadium alloys to make knife and sword blades known as Damascus steel, which were legendary for their strength and sharpness. Today, vanadium is in home toolboxes, adding durability to drill bits, wrenches, pliers, and more.

24 Cr CHROMIUM

Chromium is also known as chrome. It is hard and shiny, takes a high polish, and resists corrosion. In the 1950s and 1960s, chrome became popular as a way to create then-fashionable super-shiny metal bumpers and wheel rims on cars and motorcycles. Not only is chromium shiny in its pure form, it also prevents metal beneath it from corroding, so it is often used as a thin "plate" on top of other metals, like steel or nickel.

▲ ▲

Rainbow Connection

You might wonder why chromium gets its name from *chroma*, the Greek word for color. After all, in its pure form, it is a gray metal. But when mixed with other elements, an array of colors is produced, from dark red in chromium trioxide to rich green in chromium sesquioxide to violet in anhydrous chromium chloride. These pigments have been used since the 1700s in paints and dyes. Chromium gives gemstones like rubies, emeralds, and alexandrite their deep color.

Category: Transition metal
Year discovered: 1797
Discovered by: Nicolas-Louis Vauquelin, a French chemist
Fun fact: The pigment chrome yellow, which was made from lead chromate, was painted on American school buses until scientists discovered its toxicity. School buses are still yellow, but now they are painted with nontoxic pigments.

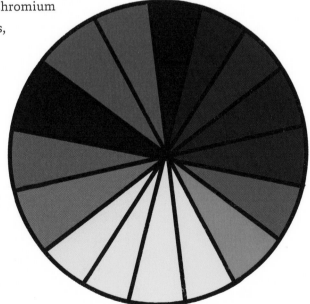

25 Mn MANGANESE

Manganese is a hard, brittle, gray metal found in a variety of minerals. It is present in seawater as manganese oxides, which have built up in layers over millions of years and form giant masses on the bed of the sea.

▲ ▲ ▲ ▲ ▲ ▲ ▲ ▲ ▲ ▲ ▲ ▲ ▲ ▲ ▲ ▲ ▲ ▲ ▲ ▲

Category: Transition metal
Year discovered: 1774
Discovered by: Johan Gottlieb Gahn, a Swedish chemist
Fun fact: Our ancestors used black manganese oxide pigments in cave paintings dating back at least seventeen thousand years.

Stronger Steel

About 90 percent of the manganese metal mined is used in the steel industry. When industry pioneers began to produce steel, they discovered that when rolled or forged, it would often break. They realized that adding small amounts of manganese to steel caused the oxygen and sulfur to disappear, which made it stronger without losing its malleability. Because of its durability, it is an alloy in train tracks and prison bars.

Does a Body Good

Some of the benefits of manganese include creating healthy bones, assisting metabolic activity, forming connective tissues, absorbing calcium, regulating blood sugar, and metabolizing fats and carbohydrates. We get our supply of manganese from eating bread, nuts, cereals, and vegetables.

ELEMENTS AND THE HUMAN BODY

Just six elements—oxygen, carbon, hydrogen, nitrogen, calcium, and phosphorus—make up 99 percent of the human body (including yours!). About 0.85 percent is composed of another five elements: potassium, sulfur, sodium, chlorine, and magnesium. The elements manganese, zinc, iodine, selenium, chromium, lithium, molybdenum, and cobalt appear in only trace amounts in our bodies but are essential to human life as well.

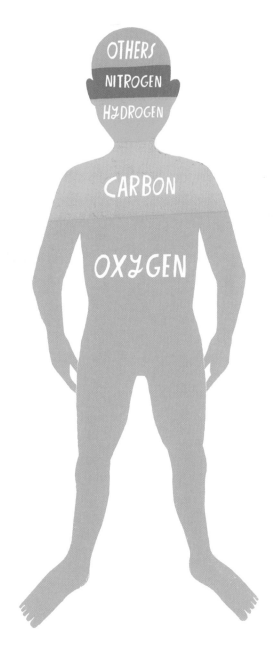

Oxygen 65%. Crucial for converting food into energy.

Carbon 18.5%. The basic building block of the cells in your body.

Hydrogen 9.5%. Helps move nutrients, remove waste, regulate body temperature, and produce energy.

Nitrogen 3.3%. Nitrogen is a key ingredient in your body's amino acids that make the proteins you need for energy.

Calcium 1.5%. Most calcium in your body makes your bones and teeth rigid and strong.

Phosphorus 1%. Your body uses phosphorus to help grow and repair cells and tissues.

Potassium 0.4%. Helps nerves process electrical signaling and maintains a balance of water in the body.

Sulfur 0.3%. Provides a place for amino acids to bond together, supporting cartilage and keratin in nails, hair, and skin.

Chlorine 0.2%. Helps with nerve transmissions and produces gastric juices.

Sodium 0.2%. Supports electrical signaling in the nervous system and regulates the amount of water in your body.

Magnesium 0.1 %. Plays an important role in the structure of your skeleton and muscles and helps get energy to cells.

26 Fe IRON

Iron has the distinction of being the most abundant and most magnetic naturally occurring element on Earth. Liquid iron makes up 80 percent of Earth's core. In its pure form, iron is a soft, gray metal. It is very reactive, and when it comes into contact with air or water, it rusts. Rust is synonymous with iron: many people associate the metal with the orangey color.

Category: Transition metal
Year discovered: Prehistoric
Discovered by: Unknown
Fun fact: There is enough iron in the Earth to make three new planets the mass of Mars.

▲ ▲

A Current Affair

Iron is responsible for Earth's magnetic field. The flow of molten iron within Earth's core creates electric currents that in turn create a magnetic field. That field reaches tens of thousands of miles into space, protecting us from charged particles in the solar wind that try to strip away Earth's atmosphere.

Iron in the Fire

Naturally occurring pure iron is found primarily in fallen meteorites! Extracting it from its ores here on Earth is called smelting. Scientists put ore containing iron in a hot furnace along with carbon (in the form of coal) and limestone. As it burns, the carbon and limestone remove the impurities from the ore, leaving behind pure iron.

Powers Put to Good Use

Because it rusts easily, iron is most useful when combined with other metals. Made more resilient as an alloy, it can be cast, machined, and welded into countless forms, which makes it one of the most useful and versatile substances on Earth. We use iron alloys to make huge structures, such as bridges, skyscrapers, and container ships, as well as cars, tools, and even paper clips!

Does a Body Good

Our bodies use iron to make hemoglobin, a substance in our blood that carries oxygen, which helps our cells produce the energy we need. If we become iron deficient, we make fewer red blood cells and can become anemic. Anemia makes people feel lethargic. We get plenty of iron from eating vegetables, grains, meat, and eggs.

A Heavenly Gift

We know that humans have used iron for at least five thousand years. In ancient times, people didn't know that iron was abundant. They thought their source of metallic iron was from meteorites that fell from the sky. Iron may have been considered desirable *because* it fell from the sky, and as such, was considered a gift from the gods. Ancient Egyptians called it the metal of heaven.

MAGNETIC
NORTH POLE

MANTLE

OUTER CORE

INNER CORE

80% IRON!

EARTH'S
MAGNETIC
FIELD

MAGNETIC
SOUTH POLE

27 Co COBALT

Cobalt is a bluish-white, hard, brittle metal. It is one of the few elements that is ferromagnetic, meaning it remains magnetized even after a magnetic field is removed. Cobalt is a catalyst, which means it is an element that facilitates a chemical reaction while it remains unchanged itself.

Category: Transition metal
Year discovered: 1735
Discovered by: Georg Brandt, a Swedish chemist
Fun fact: In ancient Egypt, cobalt blue was used to color the tomb of King Tutankhamen.

What's in a Name?

Silver miners in medieval Germany were smelting ore (heating it to extract metal) over fire when toxic fumes emerged from the oven. It turns out they were burning cobalt ore that produced cobalt-arsenic gas called cobalt arsenide, which made them sick. They became spooked and thought they had been bewitched by goblins, so they named the substance *kobold*, which is the German word for goblin. *Kobold* eventually became *cobalt*.

Radioactive for Good

Cobalt is not radioactive in its pure form, but the human-made isotope cobalt-60 releases gamma radiation. Produced artificially in nuclear reactors, it is used to treat cancer and target tumors. It is also used to sterilize medical equipment and irradiate food, a process by which food is exposed to a tiny dose of radiation to kill germs.

Feeling Blue

Ancient civilizations discovered the artistic potential of cobalt well before scientists knew much about the substance. Cobalt salts decorated pottery and other objects. Today cobalt blue, made by combining cobalt oxide with aluminum, is still a popular, fade-resistant dye, glass colorant, and paint pigment.

The Buddy System

Cobalt is a component in steel alloys, like many of its neighbors on the periodic table. Cobalt steel is one of the hardest and toughest alloys, and it is used to manufacture drills, jet plane blades, and other things that need to reach a high temperature without breaking.

NICKEL

Nickel is a hard, silvery-white metal known for its strength, resistance to heat and corrosion, ferromagnetism, and ability to be stretched into wire. All these qualities make it useful for the development of a variety of things, including cars, ships, and airplane parts, as well as coins, guitar strings, and toaster wires.

▲ ▲

Category: Transition metal
Year discovered: 1751
Discovered by: Axel Fredrik Cronstedt, a Swedish chemist
Fun fact: The U.S. five-cent coin called a nickel is actually an alloy of 75 percent copper and 25 percent nickel.

What's in a Name?

The naming of nickel in the seventeenth century is a case of mistaken identity. German miners thought they had found copper ore, but when they attempted to extract it, no copper appeared. The superstitious miners blamed "Nicholas," a demon in German mythology, for tricking them. As a result, they began calling the ore *kupfernickel*, which means "copper demon." What they had actually mined was a pale brown-red rock made of nickel and arsenic now called nickeline.

Supporting Player

Nickel often helps enhance the qualities of other metals. It is used as a protective coating for softer metals to make them more durable, and to make duller metals look more lustrous. Nickel is mixed with copper to form the alloy cupronickel, which is used as the metallic components on ships because the alloy does not corrode in seawater.

Holy Meteorite

Much of the nickel on Earth is believed to have arrived by way of humongous meteorites, one of which is thought to have been the size of Mount Everest. Scientists believe that the mountain-size, nickel-laden comet slammed into Ontario, Canada, 1.8 billion years ago.

WHAT'S IN A NAME?

There are a few elements throughout the periodic table whose symbol might make you think, "Huh, where did those letters come from?" There's usually a method to this madness. Sometimes it is representative of how the name of the element changed over time. In other instances, it is a reflection of the use of Greek and Latin names in science.

IRON

Fe is named for the Latin word for iron, *ferrum*.

SODIUM

Na is not a flippant negative reply; it is a nod to the Latin for sodium carbonate, *natrium*.

COPPER

Cu comes from the Latin word *cuprum*, meaning "from the island of Cyprus." In ancient Rome, copper was mined in Cyprus.

POTASSIUM

K is derived from *kalium*, the Medieval Latin word for *potash*, a mixture of plant ash and water, which was a common fertilizer.

SILVER

Ag is short for the Latin name for silver, *argentum*.

ANTIMONY

Sb comes from the Latin *stibium*, a term for the only mineral that contains naturally occurring antimony sulfide.

GOLD

Au, another nod to Latin, is short for the name for gold, *aurum*.

TIN

Sn is derived from the Latin *stannum*, which originally meant an alloy of silver and lead but later came to be the name for tin.

TUNGSTEN

W is a nod to wolframite, one of the ores where tungsten is found. The word *wolfram* is from the German for "wolf froth"—tin miners felt the tungsten devoured the tin during the smelting process like a wolf.

MERCURY

You may have heard mercury referred to as *quicksilver*. Its symbol **Hg** is derived from the Latin for "liquid silver," *hydrargyrum*.

LEAD

Pb is derived from another Latin term for lead, *plumbum* (also the origin of the word *plumber*).

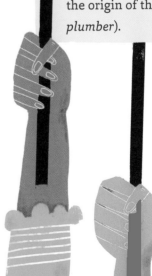

29 Cu COPPER

Copper is a soft, malleable, ductile (it can be stretched without losing its strength) metal that is an excellent conductor of heat and electricity. Copper is not particularly reactive, so it is one of the few elements found in its pure form in nature. Copper doesn't corrode, but it does react over time with the air to form a layer of copper carbonate called verdigris, which has a light green color. The Statue of Liberty is one of the copper icons covered in that green patina.

▲▲▲ ▲

Category: Transition metal
Year discovered: Prehistoric times
Discovered by: Unknown
Fun fact: There is a vast amount of copper in the top half mile (1 kilometre) of the Earth's crust—so much that at the rate we are currently extracting copper, there is enough to be mined for at least 1 million years.

The Buddy System

Copper is mixed with other metals to produce stronger alloys. Copper contributes to two important metal alloys: bronze and brass. Bronze is a combination of copper and tin, and brass is a combination of copper and zinc.

That's Ancient History

Archeologists found a copper pendant in Iraq that dates back to 8700 B.C.E., which means humans have been mining and using copper for at least ten thousand years. Archaeologists found copper tubing in a plumbing system from ancient Egypt, and it was still in excellent condition more than five thousand years later!

Powers Put to Good Use

After silver, copper has the highest electrical conductivity of any metal. Because of this, copper is used primarily to make electrical wire. Approximately 60 percent of copper is used as a conductor in electrical wiring. Copper also has antimicrobial properties. If certain bacteria come into contact with copper, they absorb copper atoms. Those atoms disrupt the bacteria's ability to function and cause them to die within a few hours of contact. Copper doorknobs help prevent the spread of infection in hospitals.

Does a Body Good

Copper is fundamental for the survival of all organisms. It combines with proteins in our bodies to produce enzymes that help our cells release energy, maintain connective tissue, and transform melanin in our skin. We get copper from eating fish, meat, nuts, and seeds.

30 Zn ZINC

Zinc is a bluish-white, lustrous metal. It is never found pure in nature, but it is found in many minerals.

▲▲▲▲▲▲▲▲▲▲▲▲▲▲▲▲▲▲▲▲▲▲

Category: Post-transition metal
Year discovered: 1746
Discovered by: Andreas Marggraf, a German chemist
Fun fact: There may be zinc in your wallet! U.S. pennies are 97.5 percent zinc and 2.5 percent copper.

Does a Body Good

Zinc is needed in the human diet. Our bodies contain more than three hundred different enzymes that rely on zinc to control our growth, digestion, immune system, and fertility. We consume zinc in red meat, cheese, oysters, brewer's yeast, and maple syrup. Conversely, zinc deficiency can stunt our growth.

Powers Put to Good Use

Zinc and oxygen create the compound zinc oxide, a white powder we use in dandruff shampoo, deodorant, makeup, and diaper rash cream. Zinc oxide absorbs ultraviolet light, making it an ingredient in sunscreen. We add zinc to rubber to make boots and tires tougher, and we use it to galvanize other metals to prevent corrosion.

31 Ga GALLIUM

Gallium is a silvery, soft metal that melts at 86° Fahrenheit (30° Celsius), which means it will become liquid if you hold it in your hand. If you could hold it, though, it would stain your skin a brown color, but don't worry: it's nontoxic.

Category: Post-transition metal
Year discovered: 1875
Discovered by: Paul-Émile Lecoq de Boisbaudran, a French chemist
Fun fact: Gallium's solid form floats on top of its liquid form (the way ice floats on water) because its liquid form is denser than the solid.

What's in a Name?

Paul-Émile Lecoq de Boisbaudran was the first to isolate gallium from a zinc ore. He named the element for his home country of France, since *Gallia* is the Latin name for France. Yet some historians believe he sneakily named the element after himself. *Le coq* is French for rooster, and *gallus* is Latin for rooster.

Powers Put to Good Use

Gallium melts near room temperature and has one of the largest liquid ranges of any metal, with a boiling point of just under 4,000° Fahrenheit (2,200° Celsius), so it is found in high-temperature thermometers used for measuring the temperature of molten metals. Gallium is in LED lights, Blu-ray lasers, spaceship solar panels, and semiconductor crystals. Gallium semiconductors operate faster than conventional silicon semiconductors and are useful in electronics and cell phones.

32 Ge GERMANIUM

Germanium was the first-ever element named after a country—in this case, Germany, the birthplace of Clemens Winkler. Germanium is a rare, silver-colored metalloid. It isn't found in its pure form in nature; it is primarily a byproduct of zinc and copper mining.

▲ ▲

Category: Metalloid
Year discovered: 1886
Discovered by: Clemens Winkler, a German chemist
Fun fact: Germanium is one of the few elements that expands when it freezes.

Light Master

Germanium dioxide mixed with glass has some cool powers. It bends light from a large area into a lens, making it possible for wide-angle camera lenses to do their job. Germanium even has a unique superpower. While it is opaque, it is transparent to invisible infrared light, which makes it fantastic for use in fiber optics, the thin, flexible glass fibers used to transmit light signals in telecommunications. In fact, combined with silicon dioxide, germanium allows infrared signals to pass unhindered through the optical fibers that connect people all over the world.

33 As ARSENIC

All forms of arsenic are poisonous to animals, but people have been attempting creative applications with the element, from decorative to medicinal, for hundreds of years. These days, its deadliness is its primary utility. Compounds of arsenic are used as rat poison and insecticides.

▲ ▲

It Ain't Easy Being Green

Before the dangers of arsenic were understood, it was used to create a vibrant green dye known as Paris Green. In the nineteenth century, designer William Morris popularized the use of the dye in wallpaper. Unfortunately, when the wallpaper was exposed to damp conditions, mold would grow and combine with the arsenic to create a toxic gas, sickening or killing the room's occupants.

Category: Metalloid
Year discovered: around 1250
Discovered by: Albertus Magnus, a German alchemist
Fun fact: Hair samples from Napoleon Bonaparte showed he had one hundred times the normal arsenic level in his system when he died in 1821. Whether he was poisoned or exposed via his environment (he is rumored to have spent his exile in a green wallpapered room) is unknown.

Napoleon Bonaparte

34 Se SELENIUM

Selenium was named after Selene, the Greek goddess of the moon. Selenium, which is rarely found in its pure form in nature, can be found in soil. Selenium happens to be in water and some foods, which is great, because we need trace amounts of it in our diet.

Category: Reactive nonmetal
Year discovered: 1817
Discovered by: Jöns Jacob Berzelius, a Swedish chemist
Fun fact: Selenium has a reputation for being a foul-smelling element on the periodic table. It's part of what makes skunk spray vile to our noses.

Does a Body Good . . . or Does It?

Yes, stinky selenium is an important nutrient to humans and animals in trace amounts, but too much has toxic effects. In the right amount, selenium helps our thyroid function properly and has antioxidant properties that help prevent cellular damage. Too much selenium causes humans to have bad breath, lose their hair, and feel nauseous and makes cows disoriented, or "loco," staring blankly or losing their sense of direction (locoweed, a plant some cows munch, can contain a lot of selenium).

Powers Put to Good Use

Selenium is used in pigments in glass and ceramics. Some selenium compounds help glass lose its hue, while others give it a rich red color. Selenium is useful in devices that respond to the intensity of light. The brighter the light, the better that selenium conducts electricity, making it useful for solar energy cells in calculators, and in light meters in cameras and photocopiers.

35 Br BROMINE

Reddish-yellow liquid bromine may smell sinister, like something you might find in the laboratory of a mad scientist, but it is a very handy element. In its pure form, bromine is reactive and one of the only elements to be liquid at room temperature. When heated to just 138° Fahrenheit (59° Celsius), it evaporates into a smelly gas with noxious fumes. In fact, bromine's name is from the Greek word for stench, *bromos*.

Category: Reactive nonmetal
Year discovered: 1826
Discovered by: Antoine-Jérôme Balard, a French chemist
Fun fact: Bromine atoms are destructive to our ozone layer. As much as half of the loss of ozone above Antarctica is due to human use of bromine.

▲ ▲

Worth Its Salt

One common use for bromine is as a disinfectant to clean swimming pools. If you jump into a pool disinfected with bromine expecting the familiar taste of chlorine, you might be confused by the salty smack to your mouth. In hot tubs, bromine works better than chlorine, because it is more stable than chlorine at warm temperatures.

Don't Play with Fire

By law in many countries, pajamas must be flame-retardant, and treating them with bromine does the trick. Get too close to a candle before bed? Never fear! Your PJ's won't erupt in flames if they contain bromine. That is because hydrobromic acid bonds with oxygen atoms, which prevents fabrics from catching fire.

Purple Rules, Bro

People have used bromide compounds since ancient times. The Romans discovered that mucus secreted by a Mediterranean snail turned purple once it met the air. It turns out that this snail's mucus was filled with bromine, which the snail absorbed from crawling on the ocean floor. The Romans began using this mucus to color their togas. Tyrian purple colored the clothing of priests and kings and was adored for its intensity and permanence.

36 Kr KRYPTON

In Greek, *kryptos* means the "hidden one." Krypton is another noble gas that hides in the background, colorless, odorless, and nonreactive with other elements. It is one of the rarest gases in our atmosphere at 1 part per million of air.

▲ ▲ ▲ ▲ ▲ ▲ ▲ ▲ ▲ ▲ ▲ ▲ ▲ ▲ ▲ ▲ ▲ ▲ ▲

Category: Noble gas
Year discovered: 1898
Discovered by: Sir William Ramsay and Morris Travers, British chemists
Fun fact: Superman's home planet of Krypton and the glowing green kryptonite that causes him to lose his powers have no association with or properties of actual krypton. It's likely that the comic book authors were just looking for a cool-sounding name.

You Light Up My Life

Like other noble gases, krypton lights up when an electric current passes through it. Krypton's glow is bright and white, ideal for use in camera flash bulbs, strobe lights, and, when combined with fluorine, lasers.

37 Rb RUBIDIUM

With a name like *rubidium*, you might think this element is ruby red. But its natural color is silver. Its name does come from the Latin word for deep red, but that's because of the prominent red lines in its spectrum. Like many of the other metals in its family, it ignites on contact with air and reacts violently with water. Because it is so reactive, scientists have to take care to store it in dry mineral oil or sealed in glass in an inert atmosphere. If you went on a rubidium hunt, you might become frustrated. It is a rare element, found in small amounts in minerals.

Category: Alkali metal
Year discovered: 1861
Discovered by: Robert Bunsen, a German chemist, and Gustav Kirchhoff, a German physicist
Fun fact: Rubidium can be used to give fireworks a purple-red color.

▲▲▲▲▲▲▲▲▲▲▲▲▲▲▲▲▲▲▲▲▲▲

Powers Put to Good Use

Rubidium's main use is in vacuum tubes (glass tubes that control electric current) as a "getter"—a material that removes trace gases from the tubes. Rubidium atoms are sensitive to light, so it is used in photoelectric cells in devices that convert light energy into electricity.

38 Sr STRONTIUM

When gray strontium touches air, it turns yellow and looks similar to gold. Because it is reactive, strontium is found embedded in other minerals.

▲ ▲

Category: Alkaline earth metal
Year discovered: 1790
Discovered by: Adair Crawford and William Cruickshank, British chemists
Fun fact: Strontium chloride is in toothpaste for sensitive teeth. It forms a barrier over areas of the tooth that are sensitive or have been exposed due to gum recession.

A Dangerous Weapon

While natural strontium is stable and harmless, the synthetic strontium-90 isotope is radioactive and was a byproduct of atomic bombs in the mid-twentieth century. Strontium-90 emits harmful radiation and is dangerous to humans. The body treats stronium-90 as if it is calcium and absorbs it into the bones, which causes cancer. However, nonradioactive strontium, like calcium, is harmless to humans and is used in supplements to strengthen bones.

The Buddy System

When partnered with other elements, strontium has several uses. Strontium aluminate creates luminous paint colors that glow in the dark because it absorbs light from its surroundings. Strontium carbonate produces red color in pyrotechnics. When you add strontium to magnets that contain iron oxide, they become stronger. These strong magnets are used in loudspeakers.

Strontium sulfate is the naturally occurring form most used to create other, more useful, strontium compounds.

39 Y YTTRIUM

Yttrium has a silver-metallic luster and is never found in its pure form in nature, though it is stable in air. Shavings of the metal ignite in air if their temperature exceeds 752° Fahrenheit (400° Celsius)—but when does it ever get that hot?

▲▲▲▲▲▲▲▲▲▲▲▲▲▲▲▲▲▲▲▲▲▲▲▲▲

Reach for the Moon

Yttrium was present in moon rock samples that astronauts on the Apollo missions brought back to Earth. Those samples contained higher levels of yttrium than rocks on Earth. Yttrium aluminum garnets (YAGs) play a role in laser technology. Powerful YAG crystals are pumped with energy and create laser lights. Those lasers cut through metal and have enough bright light to bounce to the moon and back. These lasers help us locate satellites.

Category: Transition metal
Year discovered: 1794
Discovered by: Johan Gadolin, a Finnish chemist
Fun fact: Scientists have observed more than thirty radioactive isotopes of yttrium. One of these is called Y-90, which is able to bind to cancer cells and destroy them, making it a useful tool in the treatment of cancer.

Yttrium was found in moon rock samples.

40 Zr ZIRCONIUM

The root word *zircon* comes from the Persian word *zargun*, meaning "golden," since its crystals are brownish gold. In its pure state, zirconium is silvery white.

▲ ▲

Category: Transition metal
Year discovered: 1789
Discovered by: Martin Heinrich Klaproth, a German chemist
Fun fact: Zircon sand covers entire beaches in Australia.

Shine Bright Like a Diamond

Zirconium is famous for its dubious distinction as a convincing "fake diamond." Cubic zirconium gems sparkle because they display a high refractive index. When light enters zirconium, it is trapped and bounces around inside the gem. When light escapes from the gem, it releases in a range of directions, making the gem sparkle.

Tough Stuff

When you heat powdered zirconium oxide, it produces a hard, glass-like ceramic that is resistant to corrosion and heat. In fact, this compound doesn't melt until it reaches 4,919° Fahrenheit (2,715° Celsius)! It is in things that need to be super strong, such as dental crowns, golf clubs, spacecraft, and jet engine turbine blades.

Neutron-Resistant

Zirconium is used in the interior of nuclear reactors. One of zirconium's superpowers is that it doesn't absorb neutrons, making it an ideal material for the pipes inside reactors that house nuclear fission (a process by which the nucleus of an atom splits into smaller parts, releasing energy and free neutrons). The free neutrons pass right through zirconium without it becoming radioactive.

41 Nb NIOBIUM

Niobium is a soft, silver metal, which has a few handy powers. For one, it does not expand in high heat, so we use it in jet engine parts, gas turbines, and rocket components. It is resistant to corrosion and used to create pacemakers, surgical instruments, and jewelry that go inside or touch the human body.

Category: Transition metal
Year discovered: 1801
Discovered by: Charles Hatchett, a British chemist
Fun fact: Niobium has fantastic superconductive properties, making it useful in superconductive magnets for MRI equipment and mass spectrometers.

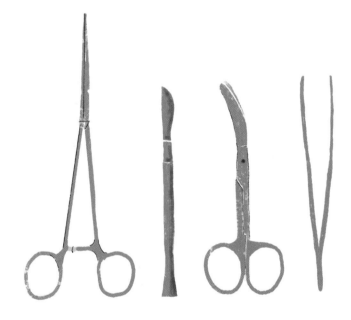

Origin Story

Charles Hatchett discovered niobium when he was experimenting with the mineral columbite. First, he heated niobium with potassium carbonate and dissolved it in water. Then he added acid to form an oxide powder. The solid that emerged intrigued him, and he thought it might be a new element. Fellow scientists doubted whether this new element wasn't tantalum, which was discovered around the same time, also from columbite. These elements are so similar that scientists were confused for years. But in 1844, German chemist Heinrich Rose proved once and for all that the columbite mineral contained both tantalum and niobium, and that they were indeed different elements.

42 Mo MOLYBDENUM

Molybdenum is a mouthful to say, but this obscure element has many practical uses. It gets it unusual name from the Greek word *molybdos*, which means "lead." Miners once mistook the dark mineral for lead, but molybdenum is much harder than lead.

▲ ▲

Powers Put to Good Use

Molybdenum can withstand high temperatures, and it is slippery and lightweight. You will find it mixed with other metals in bicycle frames, cars, aircraft, and rockets. Ground into a fine powder and mixed with oil, it produces a slippery lubricant, used in fast-moving mechanical engine parts.

Does a Body Good

Although it is toxic in anything other than small quantities, molybdenum is a crucial element in all species, playing a role in how we metabolize (convert to energy) our food. Molybdenum enters our diet through the plants we eat, which absorb it from the soil.

Category: Transition metal
Year discovered: 1781
Discovered by: Carl Wilhelm Scheele and Peter Jacob Hjelm, Swedish chemists
Fun fact: The Russian space program's Luna 24 mission collected molybdenum samples from the moon.

43 Tc TECHNETIUM

Technetium's significant claim to fame is that it was the first element to be artificially produced by scientists, in this case by Segrè and Perrier, a pair of chemists. It is even named for the Greek word for artificial, *technetos*. Since every isotope of technetium is very unstable and all decay very quickly, it is not surprising that it is exceedingly rare on Earth (only very minute quantities have been found). Astronomers who study the spectral lines (wavelengths seen as colored lines emitted by every element) have found trace amounts of technetium in stars.

Category: Transition metal
Year discovered: 1937
Discovered by: Emilio Segrè, an Italian-American physicist, and Carlo Perrier, an Italian chemist
Fun fact: Technetium was the first element to be artificially produced.

▲ ▲

Lifesaving Exposure

The radioactive isotope technetium-99, when added to an immune system protein, binds with cancer cells and emits gamma rays. It is used in medical imaging to detect cancerous growths, blood clots, and other abnormalities.

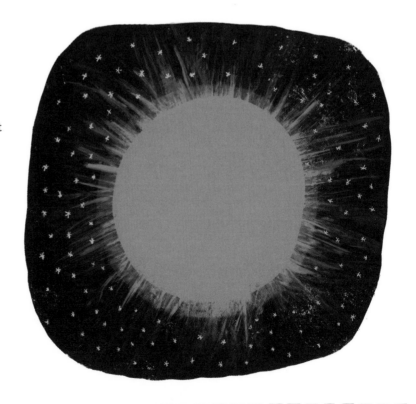

Technetium has been detected in red giant stars.

44 Ru RUTHENIUM

Named for the Latin word for Russia, where it was first unearthed, ruthenium is one of the rarest metals on the planet. It belongs to the prestigious platinum group metals (PGMs), a family of expensive elements on the periodic table. Superstars in their own right, PGMs are both rare and useful. Ruthenium itself is valuable because it is unaffected by air, water, or acid, so it is highly resistant to corrosion.

Category: Transition metal
Year discovered: 1844
Discovered by: Karl Karlovich Klaus, a Russian chemist
Fun fact: Ruthenium has certain light-absorbing qualities that make it ideal for use in solar energy cells.

▲ ▲

Powers Put to Good Use

Tough and beautiful, ruthenium is useful in jewelry making. It is used as thin plating on other metals to give them luster. It is also a catalyst for industrial processes, such as electrical circuits, chip resistors, and high-capacity magnetic hard drives.

The Parker 51 fountain pen was outfitted with a 14-karat-gold nib tipped with 96.2 percent ruthenium.

OLIVER SACKS: COLLECTOR OF ELEMENTS

Did you know that there are people whose hobby is to collect elements from the periodic table? Many collectors enjoy the challenge of finding the elements, much like going on a scavenger hunt. One well-known element collector was famed neurologist and writer Oliver Sacks.

Sacks was fascinated by the elements from the time he was a young boy. He tells the story of his fascination in his book *Uncle Tungsten*. By the time he was in his late seventies, his fascination reached an all-time high. His home was even decorated with references from the periodic table, including periodic table cushions and a periodic table comforter on his bed!

Best of all, he had a wooden box in his living room that contained ninety elements, all organized into tiny glass vials, and ordered in the box like the periodic table. Over the years, his friends sent him elements for his collection as birthday presents.

Sacks considered the elements his friends. He loved that they made up everything in the universe. Some of them were things he could hold in his hands, some of them were dangerous, and some could do exciting things, like explode on contact with other elements.

Friends would give Sacks elements for his collection to commemorate his birthdays. He received a piece of hafnium (element number 72) on his seventy-second birthday and a smooth slab of iridium (element number 77) on his seventy-seventh birthday.

45 Rh RHODIUM

Like its siblings in the precious metal group, rhodium is hard, silvery white, and resistant to corrosion. Rhodium is also rare, and it is more valuable than platinum or gold. In fact, it is more than one hundred times rarer than gold! It is unaffected by air or water up to 1,112° Fahrenheit (600° Celsius) and impervious to acid, too—up to 212° Fahrenheit (100° Celsius). Molten alkalis are some of the only substances that can break down this precious metal.

Category: Transition metal
Year discovered: 1803
Discovered by: William Hyde Wollaston, a British chemist
Fun fact: In 1979, the *Guinness Book of World Records* presented singer, songwriter, and former Beatle Paul McCartney a rhodium-plated disc to celebrate his status as the most successful songwriter in history.

▲ ▲

Always a Bridesmaid, Never a Bride

You might wonder, if rhodium is rare, beautiful, and robust, why isn't it as famous as gold or platinum? The answer is because it is too scarce and expensive to be used on its own and is instead usually alloyed with its sibling metals, platinum and palladium.

Powers Put to Good Use

Rhodium is only rarely used in jewelry, but it is a key ingredient with platinum and palladium in catalytic converters (a device that converts pollutants from engines into less toxic emissions). It is also employed as a coating for optical fibers and mirrors in the reflectors of car headlights. Rhodium's ultimate superpower? It has a particular ability to absorb oxygen from the atmosphere without becoming oxidized itself.

THE ROLE OF ELEMENTS IN CATALYTIC CONVERTERS

We rely on cars, buses, and trucks to help us move from place to place in a quick and efficient manner. But the emissions caused by vehicle exhaust release dangerous hydrocarbons, carbon monoxide, and nitrogen oxide into the air that can harm people, plants, and animals, as well as the planet. Fortunately, vehicles are now fitted with pollution-reducing units called catalytic converters, and a few key elements of the periodic table have a role in making catalytic converters work.

Catalytic converters convert harmful gases that vehicles emit to relatively harmless atoms. Catalytic converters split up the molecules after they leave a vehicle's engine. Platinum, palladium, or rhodium act as "catalysts" in catalytic converters. These elements break apart the toxic gases and convert them to gases that are safe enough to blow into the air.

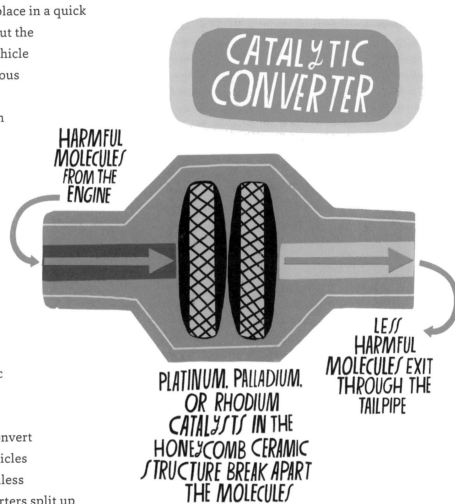

CATALYTIC CONVERTER

HARMFUL MOLECULES FROM THE ENGINE

LESS HARMFUL MOLECULES EXIT THROUGH THE TAILPIPE

PLATINUM, PALLADIUM, OR RHODIUM CATALYSTS IN THE HONEYCOMB CERAMIC STRUCTURE BREAK APART THE MOLECULES

46 Pd PALLADIUM

Like its platinum group metal sibling rhodium, palladium is rare and valuable among all the metals. It is thirty times rarer than gold. Palladium is found in nature alloyed with gold or other platinum group metals throughout the world.

Category: Transition metal
Year discovered: 1803
Discovered by: William Hyde Wollaston, a British chemist
Fun fact: Palladium is malleable, and like gold it can be beaten into leaves as thin as a micrometer.

Powers Put to Good Use

Palladium's rarity and malleability, along with its tendency not to tarnish, make it a good fit for precious jewelry. It is alloyed with gold to make the popular white gold. However, palladium's main contribution is as a key ingredient in catalytic converters, helping the devices convert pollutants from cars into carbon dioxide and water.

Disappearing Act

One of the incredible qualities of palladium is its ability to absorb hydrogen gas. A solid piece of palladium absorbs nine hundred times its volume in gas, which disappears into the solid metal. You might ask, how is this even possible? When a hydrogen molecule meets the surface of palladium, it breaks down into its component atoms and sneaks in between the palladium atoms. If it weren't so rare and expensive, palladium would be an effective way to store hydrogen.

A ball of pure palladium

SILVER

Silver has been mined since 3000 B.C.E. and has been prized for coins, tableware, jewelry, and ornaments for at least five thousand years. It is one of the least chemically reactive of the transition metals, but it still needs a regular polish or protective coating to maintain a shine. Its shine is brilliant enough to make it the most reflective of the metals and ideal for mirrors. Silver is the best conductor of heat and electricity of any element, but its high cost to mine means that most electrical wire is copper, not silver.

▲ ▲

Category: Transition metal
Year discovered: Approximately 3000 B.C.E.
Discovered by: Unknown
Fun fact: Just 0.035 ounces (1 gram) of silver can be stretched into a wire of more than 1.25 miles (2 kilometres) in length!

Setting the Table

People began using silver utensils because it left less of a metallic taste in the mouth than other metals. Pure silver is too soft for flatware, so copper is added to create sterling silver. These days flatware is made from stainless steel, which is more economical and less susceptible to tarnish.

Another Silver Lining

Like copper, silver ions have a toxic effect on bacteria and viruses. Silver nitrate is in disinfectants and in antibacterial soaps. Sometimes silver thread is woven into socks to kill the microbes associated with stinky feet.

48 Cd CADMIUM

Cadmium is a soft, silvery, toxic metal. Like mercury and lead, it can accumulate in the body and environment, creating long-term health and ecological damages. Cadmium's primary contribution to humankind (outside of art) has been in nickel-cadmium batteries. Because they were rechargeable, cadmium batteries were thought of as an environmental solution, but we now have more powerful, and less toxic, rechargeable battery alternatives.

▲ ▲

Ouch-Ouch

Continued exposure to cadmium leaches calcium deposits from bones, leaving the bones brittle and the joints painful. In Japan in the early twentieth century, a community grew ill from eating rice grown in fields rich in cadmium salts. They called the disease *itai-itai*, which translates to "ouch-ouch."

Category: Post-transition metal
Year discovered: 1817
Discovered by: Friedrich Stromeyer, a German chemist
Fun fact: One of the paints favored by Claude Monet was brilliant cadmium yellow. Television painting instructor Bob Ross was also a fan of cadmium yellow, dabbing it on his "happy trees." Cadmium has fallen out of favor in artists' paints due to its toxicity.

49 In INDIUM

Indium is named for the deep blue indigo light it emits when electrified. A bar of pure indium is so soft that you could cut it with a knife, but when combined with other metals, indium gets stronger.

▲ ▲

Category: Post-transition metal
Year discovered: 1863
Discovered by: Ferdinand Reich and Hieronymous Richter, German chemists
Fun fact: Indium "screams" when it is bent. Really! The crystals in the metal break and rearrange, emitting a high-pitched shriek.

The Magic Touch

Due to an initial lack of practical uses for the element, at the turn of the twentieth century, there was less than 2.2 pounds (1 kilogram) of pure indium worldwide. Today, hundreds of tons are refined each year. Most indium production goes into the compound indium tin oxide (ITO). ITO is transparent to light but able to conduct electricity. ITO is the technology behind LCD (liquid crystal display) televisions and is part of the touch-screen technology in our phones. Some scientists estimate that we may run out of indium in the next few decades based on our current consumption rates, making recycling efforts essential.

 **TIN**

Tin was one of the first metals used by humans. Five thousand years ago, humans began to mix tin with copper, creating the stronger alloy bronze, ushering in the Bronze Age of durable weaponry and elaborate artistry. Today, tin continues to be used to create tough metal alloys like bronze and pewter. You will find it coated on other metals to prevent rust.

▲ ▲

Chilly Transformation

In cold temperatures, tin will change from a silvery metal into a dark gray powder over time. This transformation is not a chemical reaction but an actual change in the crystal structure of the metal. It is rumored that the tin buttons on Napoleon's army's uniforms began to turn to powder when exposed to the frigid temperatures in Russia, causing soldiers to get hypothermia when they could no longer button their coats.

Category: Post-transition metal
Year discovered: Approximately 2100 B.C.E.
Discovered by: Unknown
Fun fact: Many things called "tin"—foil, cans, roofs, and so on—are not actually made from tin. The element's name has become a catchall term for any thin sheet metal.

51 Sb ANTIMONY

Antimony gets its name from the Greek *anti-monos*, meaning "not alone." It is true that the element is rarely found on its own in nature—it is almost always a compound with other heavier metals. The mineral ore stibnite is the largest source of antimony and the origin of its symbol, *Sb*.

▲ ▲

Category: Metalloid
Year discovered: Approximately 1600 B.C.E.
Discovered by: Unknown
Fun fact: The distinctive dark kohl eye makeup of ancient Egyptians was made from powdered antimony-rich ore.

The Right Type

Combined with lead and tin, antimony creates an alloy that is perfect for pouring into molds for letterpress type. This "movable type" was popularized in the fifteenth century by Johannes Gutenberg and became the standard for printing presses for more than five hundred years.

Bad Medicine

Despite being as poisonous as arsenic to humans, antimony has a long history of medicinal uses, usually as an emetic (something that makes you throw up). It was wrongly believed that this purging would cleanse the body of disease. Some have speculated that one of these antimony remedies may have been the cause of composer Wolfgang Amadeus Mozart's death.

Egyptian kohl eye makeup

52 Te TELLURIUM

One of the rarest elements on Earth, tellurium is produced as a sludge byproduct from copper and lead mining. However, 500 *tons* (454 tonnes) of copper must be refined to acquire 1 pound (0.45 kilograms) of tellurium!

▲ ▲ ▲ ▲ ▲ ▲ ▲ ▲ ▲ ▲ ▲ ▲ ▲ ▲ ▲ ▲ ▲ ▲

Category: Metalloid
Year discovered: 1783
Discovered by: Franz Joseph Müller von Reichenstein, an Austrian mineralogist
Fun fact: While tellurium is considered to be mildly toxic to humans, ingesting even a tiny amount can leave you with super stinky breath and body odor for weeks.

Powers Put to Good Use

Tellurium has a wide range of technical applications, from fiber optic cables to the reflective layer of DVD disks that allows information to be written by lasers. It plays a key role in solar power technology. Panels coated in an alloy of cadmium and tellurium harness energy from the sun.

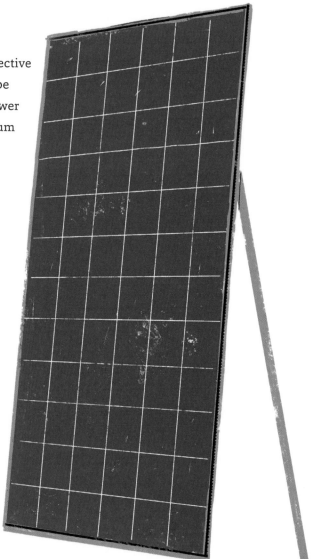

Solar panel

53 I IODINE

Solid at room temperature, exposed iodine slowly turns into a gas without pausing for a moment to become a liquid! Most elemental solids are silvery or gray, but iodine is blue-black when solid, and as a gas it is vivid violet. In fact, its name is derived from the Greek word for violet, *iodes*.

Category: Reactive nonmetal
Year discovered: 1811
Discovered by: Bernard Courtois, a French chemist
Fun fact: So essential is iodine to human health that, starting in 1924, it has been added to table salt to ensure it's in everyone's diet.

▲ ▲ ▲ ▲ ▲ ▲ ▲ ▲ ▲ ▲ ▲ ▲ ▲ ▲ ▲ ▲ ▲

Regulation Monitor

Iodine is important to the well-being of humans and animals. Metabolic functions like body temperature and hormone levels are regulated by iodine, and having the right amount is key. People who produce too much thyroid hormone (in which iodine is a key component) have hyperthyroidism, which causes restlessness, weight loss, heat intolerance, and difficulty concentrating. People who do not produce enough thyroid hormone can get an enlarged thyroid gland, called hypothyroidism. It causes fatigue, cold intolerance, weight gain, and dry skin.

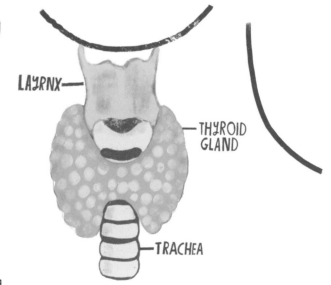

LAYRNX

THYROID GLAND

TRACHEA

Medical Marvel

A powerful antimicrobial (germ-killing) agent, iodine is used to purify water and as an antiseptic to treat wounds. It is the active ingredient in the yellow-brown disinfectant paste painted onto patients before surgery. Radioactive iodine therapy destroys thyroid tissue or cancer cells, aiding in the treatment of thyroid cancer.

54 Xe XENON

Although not common in the Earth's atmosphere, xenon is a noble gas that you might see in use on a daily basis. Incandescent light bulbs filled with xenon burn hot and bright, making them ideal for car headlights.

▲ ▲

Category: Noble gas
Year discovered: 1898
Discovered by: Sir William Ramsay and Morris Travers, British chemists
Fun fact: While there are just traces of xenon in our atmosphere, it is present in abundance in Jupiter's atmosphere.

Don't Be a Stranger

Xenon's name comes from *xenon*, Greek for "stranger." Like other noble gases, it was once thought xenon was inert and nonreactive, but in the 1960s scientists at the University of British Columbia discovered that xenon does form some compounds with other elements, including xenon oxides that are highly explosive.

Getting Your Xeeeeees

Xenon gas is nontoxic to humans and will put you safely to sleep with few side effects. Xenon has not commonly been used as an anesthetic because it is expensive, but new recycling techniques may make it more cost-effective for surgery.

JUPITER

55 Cs CESIUM

Cesium is the most reactive metal on Earth. It will explode upon contact with water. Laboratories store cesium in sealed glass vials with the air removed to prevent such explosions. Rare on Earth, it is extracted from the mineral pollucite, but it is also a byproduct of nuclear fission in reactors.

▲ ▲

Category: Alkali metal
Year discovered: 1860
Discovered by: Gustav Kirchhoff, a German physicist, and Robert Bunsen, a German chemist
Fun fact: Cesium is named for the Latin word for sky blue, *caesius*, due to its blue spectral lines.

Timekeeper

Despite its explosive nature, cesium's primary use is steady and paced. Cesium atomic clocks measure time down to a billionth of a second. A mechanical clock measures time by tracking a pendulum swinging back and forth. Atomic clocks measure time by the resonance—the jumping back and forth—of the electrons in cesium atoms at an exact frequency. Atomic clocks send signals all over the world, standardizing time for the Internet, cellular phone networks, and satellite navigation systems.

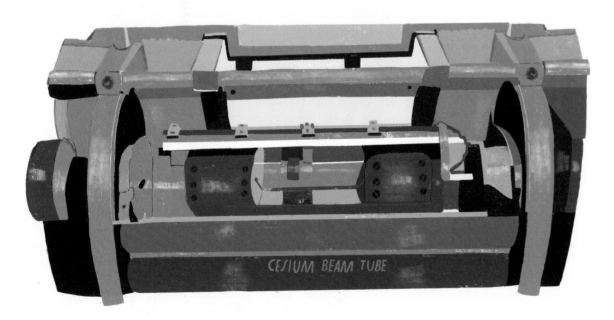

Cesium atomic clock

56 Ba BARIUM

Barium, named for the Greek word for heavy, isn't actually dense; it is lighter than titanium, which is known for being lightweight. However, barium *compounds* are usually quite dense and do a lot of heavy work.

▲ ▲

Hard to Swallow, Easy to See

A common use of barium is as a barium sulfate compound liquid that patients drink so doctors can get a look at their digestive tract. Nontoxic because it doesn't dissolve in water, opaque to X-rays, and dense enough that it moves quickly into the stomach, the barium solution helps illuminate problems within the digestive system as seen through X-ray images. The same density that moves barium sulfate through the twists and turns of your body benefits oil well mining, too, where the compound sinks into drill holes to help remove debris.

Category: Alkaline earth metal
Year discovered: 1808
Discovered by: Sir Humphry Davy, a British chemist
Fun fact: The barium-rich mineral barite glows after exposure to light.

57 La LANTHANUM

Lanthanum, a soft, silvery-white metal, has no use in its pure form, but when alloyed with other metals, it plays many roles. Mixed with nickel, it is perfect for storing hydrogen gas for hydrogen-powered vehicles. Also, that hybrid car down the street contains 22 to 33 pounds (10 to 15 kilograms) of lanthanum in the electrodes of its batteries. Lanthanum oxide is used in making special optical glass for cameras and telescopes.

Category: Lanthanoid
Year discovered: 1839
Discovered by: Carl Gustaf Mosander, a Swedish chemist
Fun fact: In the late 1800s, lanthanum was used in green-glowing lanterns that hung outside businesses.

▲ ▲ ▲ ▲ ▲ ▲ ▲ ▲ ▲ ▲ ▲ ▲ ▲ ▲ ▲ ▲ ▲ ▲ ▲

58 Ce CERIUM

Cerium is the second element of the lanthanoid series and as common as copper. Cerium is pyrophoric, which means when you scratch or grind it, its shavings catch fire—making it a common ingredient in lighter flints. You will find it on television and film sets, as it creates sparks in special effects. Cerium can be found in engines as a purification catalyst in catalytic converters, lowering the amount of harmful fumes released into the atmosphere.

Category: Lanthanoid
Year discovered: 1803
Discovered by: Jöns Jacob Berzelius and Wilhelm Hisinger, Swedish chemists, and independently by Martin Heinrich Klaproth, a German chemist
Fun fact: Cerium is named after the dwarf planet Ceres, which was discovered two years before the element.

▲ ▲ ▲ ▲ ▲ ▲ ▲ ▲ ▲ ▲ ▲ ▲ ▲ ▲ ▲ ▲ ▲ ▲

59 Pr PRASEODYMIUM

Praseodymium is a soft, malleable gray metal. It is named for *prasios*, the Greek word for green, because it forms a green coating when it comes in contact with air, and *didymos*, the word for twin. It was one of two elements to be extracted from didymium (the other is neodymium), which scientists first thought was a single element. Auer von Welsbach confirmed that it was actually two elements in 1885.

Category: Lanthanoid
Year discovered: 1885
Discovered by: Carl Auer von Welsbach, an Austrian scientist
Fun fact: Praseodymium compounds make excellent magnets. They are used in magnetic chillers, machines that can cool material down to within a few millionths of absolute zero (-459° Fahrenheit/-273° Celsius).

Easy on the Eyes

Welders and glassblowers rely on praseodymium for eye protection. A mixture of this element and its twin, neodymium, is used in the glass of welder's goggles, protecting the welder's eyes from the intense light of the flame. When wearing the goggles, the welder sees nothing but the dull blue glow of the torch and the orange glow of the hot glass or metal. Without these goggles, the yellow light would be blinding.

60 Nd NEODYMIUM

Neodymium is praseodymium's twin and was named for the Greek words for "new twin." Its impressive claim is its role in high-powered magnets. In 1983, scientists discovered that when neodymium is alloyed with iron and boron, it has a magnetic force that is powerful enough that a few grams of the magnet can lift and hold one thousand times its own weight! The combination of these three elements allows them to store impressive amounts of magnetic energy, while at the same time remaining resistant to demagnetization. They are ubiquitous in things that require a strong but lightweight magnet: laptop computers, cell phones, headphones, handheld drills, and wind turbines. Hybrid and electric vehicles use high-strength neodymium magnets to power their motors.

Category: Lanthanoid
Year discovered: 1885
Discovered by: Carl Auer von Welsbach, an Austrian scientist
Fun fact: The attraction between two neodymium magnets is so intense that if placed close enough together, they can collide and shatter.

61 Pm PROMETHIUM

Promethium is the rarest lanthanoid. Any promethium that was originally in Earth's rocks decayed billions of years ago, because it is so reactive. Only tiny trace amounts exist on Earth now, formed by the radioactive decay of other elements and existing briefly before it decays itself. It was named for the Greek god Prometheus, who stole fire from the heavens. Now produced artificially in nuclear reactors, promethium has few uses beyond research. A tiny bit is in pin-size atomic batteries that power pacemakers, guided missiles, and radios.

Category: Lanthanoid
Year discovered: 1945
Discovered by: Jacob A. Marinsky, Lawrence E. Glendenin, and Charles D. Coryell, American scientists
Fun fact: Promethium salts are radioactive and glow in the dark with a blue or green hue.

62 Sm SAMARIUM

Samarium is named after the mineral samarskite, from which it was first mined. In its pure metallic form, samarium is silvery white and lustrous. When it is alloyed with cobalt, samarium makes a fantastic permanent magnet in electric guitars. Samarian cobalt magnets sense vibrations produced by guitar strings. Some of the strongest magnets on Earth, samarian cobalt magnets remain magnetic at high temperatures.

Category: Lanthanoid
Year discovered: 1879
Discovered by: Paul-Émile Lecoq de Boisbaudran, a French chemist
Fun fact: The headphones of the first portable cassette player, the Sony Walkman, used samarium cobalt magnets.

63 Eu EUROPIUM

Europium is a soft metal, silver in color. Like francium and scandium, europium is named after a place, in this case, Europe. It is an interesting choice for a name, since much of the world's europium comes from the United States and China.

Category: Lanthanoid
Year discovered: 1901
Discovered by: Eugène-Anatole Demarçay, a French chemist
Fun fact: Europium was found in moon rock samples.

The europium oxide in this withdrawn British £50 note glows under ultraviolet light.

Seeing Red

Europium is rare, as lanthanoids go. Only 110 tons (100 tonnes) of Europium is produced each year. Before the LED flat-screen TVs we have today, cathode ray tubes inside of television sets fired electrons at a glass screen painted with chemicals that emitted light, and europium provided the red color. Today, europium's power to give off a red light makes it a great addition to fluorescent light bulbs, where red softens the usual harsh white of fluorescent strip lighting. A compound called europium oxide is used in Euro and British banknotes. When placed under ultraviolet light, the compound gives off a red glow, distinguishing real bills from counterfeit ones.

64 Gd GADOLINIUM

A soft and silvery metal, gadolinium has contrasting magnetic properties. Below 68° Fahrenheit (20° Celsius), it is attracted to a magnet (ferromagnetic); above 68° Fahrenheit (20° Celsius), the magnetic properties disappear. Gadolinium compounds are used to help produce clear images inside of a magnetic resonance imaging scanner (MRI). Patients are injected with a gadolinium compound that the body absorbs, thus enhancing the scan of the human body.

Category: Lanthanoid
Year discovered: 1880
Discovered by: Jean-Charles Galissard de Marignac and Paul-Émile Lecoq de Boisbaudran, French chemists
Fun fact: Gadolinium is magnetocaloric, which means its temperature goes up when it is placed in a magnetic field and goes down when it is removed from the field.

65 Tb TERBIUM

Terbium is silvery white and malleable. Like europium, terbium is used in cathode-ray tubes in computer monitors and TV screens, giving off a green color. Alloyed with neodymium and dysprosium, terbium has been used in the magnets that help power hybrid cars and wind turbines.

Category: Lanthanoid
Year discovered: 1843
Discovered by: Carl Gustaf Mosander, a Swedish chemist
Fun fact: The radioactive isotope terbium-149 can be used to treat cancer. Targeted at the cancer cells' receptors, the radiation kills the cancer cells, but without spreading too far, leaving healthy cells undamaged.

66 Dy DYSPROSIUM

Paul-Émile Lecoq de Boisbaudran worked hard to obtain dysprosium, trying thirty-two times to isolate it with ammonia and then twenty-six times with oxalate salts. Because of his efforts, he named the element for the Greek word *dysprositos*, which means "hard to get." Scientists weren't able to isolate the element into a purer form until around 1950, seventy-five years after it was discovered. Its magnetic strength makes it useful in data storage, computer hard disks, and electric vehicle batteries.

▲ ▲ ▲ ▲ ▲ ▲ ▲ ▲ ▲ ▲ ▲ ▲ ▲ ▲ ▲ ▲ ▲ ▲

Category: Lanthanoid
Year discovered: 1886
Discovered by: Paul-Émile Lecoq de Boisbaudran, a French chemist
Fun fact: A dysprosium alloy known as Terfenol-D visibly lengthens and shortens when it is exposed to a magnetic field.

67 Ho HOLMIUM

Named after the Swedish city of Stockholm, holmium is exceptional because it has the highest "magnetic moment" of all the elements on the periodic table. The magnetic moment quantifies the force a magnetic substance can exert. When a material with a strong magnetic moment is placed in a magnetic field, all of its atoms line up with the field. For this reason, holmium is used to make pole pieces for magnets.

▲ ▲ ▲ ▲ ▲ ▲ ▲ ▲ ▲ ▲ ▲ ▲ ▲

Category: Lanthanoid
Year discovered: 1878
Discovered by: Marc Delafontaine and Jacques-Louis Soret, Swiss chemists, and later independently by Per Teodor Cleve, a Swedish chemist
Fun fact: Holmium oxide is used to give both glass and cubic zirconia a red or yellow hue.

68 Er ERBIUM

Like its lanthanoid siblings, erbium is soft and silver, doesn't occur in its pure form in nature, and reacts with both oxygen (although slowly) and water. Erbium helps connect the world. When we send data through the Internet, we use pulses of light through fiber optic cables. Sending data over long distances would be difficult without erbium, which amplifies weak signals traveling through cables.

▲▲ ▲▲▲▲▲ ▲ ▲▲ ▲▲▲ ▲ ▲▲▲ ▲▲ ▲▲ ▲▲

Category: Lanthanoid
Year discovered: 1843
Discovered by: Carl Gustaf Mosander, a Swedish chemist
Fun fact: Three different elements are named after the Swedish village of Ytterby, where they were all discovered: erbium, terbium, and ytterbium.

69 Tm THULIUM

Soft, silvery thulium, not to be confused with thallium (element 81), is one of the least abundant of all the lanthanoid metals and is considered to be one of the least useful as well. But that doesn't mean it doesn't have a few contributions. It is a component of the lasers that are used by surgeons to cut away damaged tissue. One of its radioactive isotopes emits X-rays and can be used in lightweight, portable X-ray machines.

▲▲▲▲▲ ▲▲▲▲ ▲ ▲▲ ▲ ▲▲▲ ▲▲ ▲ ▲▲

Category: Lanthanoid
Year discovered: 1879
Discovered by: Per Teodor Cleve, a Swedish chemist

Surgical laser

70 Yb YTTERBIUM

Of all the lanthanoids, this soft and silvery-white metal is the most reactive. For an obscure metal, it has a few important jobs. It is a component in some of the world's atomic clocks, which are so precise that they can even measure the slowing of time caused by gravity! Ytterbium is added to steel to make it stronger, and to lasers and X-ray machines.

Category: Lanthanoid
Year discovered: 1878
Discovered by: Jean-Charles Galissard de Marignac, a Swiss chemist
Fun fact: Ytterbium works well under pressure; it is used in gauges underground to measure places in the Earth that have been deformed by earthquakes and explosions.

71 Lu LUTETIUM

Lutetium has the highest melting point of all the rare earth metals. And it is the hardest and densest element in the lanthanoid family. But for all its cool attributes, lutetium is rare and has a few uses, mainly mixed with crude oil in refineries to break it down for gasoline and diesel fuel.

Category: Lanthanoid
Year discovered: 1907
Discovered by: Georges Urbain, a French chemist, Carl Auer von Welsbach, an Austrian chemist, and Charles James, an American chemist
Fun fact: Lutetium was once the most expensive element on the periodic table. Scientists have now discovered more effective ways of extracting it, and the price has gone down.

72 Hf HAFNIUM

Hafnium's discovery came late, as it was difficult to separate it from zirconium. The two are nearly identical chemically, but zirconium is transparent to neutrons, where hafnium absorbs them. In a nuclear reaction, neutron particles collide. Neutron-absorber hafnium is used in control rods to help control the reactions. Hafnium is resistant to heat and corrosion and is used in plasma welding and microchips.

Category: Transition metal
Year discovered: 1923
Discovered by: George Charles de Hevesy, a Hungarian chemist, and Dirk Coster, a Dutch physicist
Fun fact: Hafnium is named after *Hafnia*, the Latin for *Copenhagen*, the city of its discovery.

▲ ▲

73 Ta TANTALUM

The hard, silvery metal tantalum proved so elusive to isolate that it was named for the legendary Greek figure Tantalus, king of Sipylus. Tantalus, after stealing the food of the gods and sacrificing his own son (and serving him up at a banquet!), was condemned to be forever tormented by thirst and hunger. He was forced to stand in a pool of water with fruit branches just out of his grasp. Water would rise up to his neck that would then recede each time he tried to drink, and tantilizing fresh fruit swayed out of his every reach.

Category: Transition metal
Year discovered: 1802
Discovered by: Anders Gustav Ekeberg, a Swedish chemist
Fun fact: While Ekeberg thought he had discovered a new metal in 1802, another chemist was convinced it was the same element as niobium. It wasn't until forty years later that scientists confirmed the two different elements were distinct.

▲ ▲

Powers Put to Good Use

Our mobile phones and other small electronics benefit from capacitors made from tantalum. Tantalum is also nontoxic and tolerated by human bodies, so it is used to make artificial joints and other body implants.

Risky Business

Tantalum ore can be found in the Democratic Republic of Congo. Tantalum mining has been disastrous for wildlife there, especially for gorillas, which are hunted for food in order to support the influx of miners to the remote area.

74 W TUNGSTEN

Category: Transition metal
Year discovered: 1783
Discovered by: Juan Elhuyar and Fausto Elhuyar, Spanish chemists
Fun fact: Tungsten has nearly the same density as gold, but not its yellow glint. Counterfeiters would coat bricks of tungsten in a layer of gold in order to pass them off as gold bars.

Tungsten is a tough element. It is quite dense and almost impossible to melt. A strong metal at high temperatures, tungsten became the choice for incandescent light bulb manufacturing, although tungsten filaments do a poor job of converting electricity to light because much of the energy is converted to heat, not light.

Tough Enough

The compound tungsten carbide is one of the hardest and strongest available. It toughens everything from drill bits to saw blades to the tips of ballpoint pens.

75 Re RHENIUM

Category: Transition metal
Year discovered: 1925
Discovered by: Walter Noddack, Ida Noddack, and Otto Carl Berg, German chemists
Fun fact: When Mendeleev designed the periodic table, he predicted and left a space for rhenium. It was the last stable element to be discovered.

Rhenium is one of the rarest elements on Earth. Its high melting point and density make it an attractive addition to metal alloys, but its scarcity limits how much we can use. Metals alloyed with rhenium can withstand extreme temperatures and are used in the engines of fighter planes.

76 Os OSMIUM

Category: Transition metal
Year discovered: 1803
Discovered by: Smithson Tennant, a British chemist

Toxic and volatile with oxygen in its pure form, osmium is used only as an alloy. Hard and strong, osmium metal alloys were found to be perfect for the needles of vinyl record players and the nibs of fountain pens because of their density.

▲▲▲▲▲▲▲▲▲▲▲▲▲▲▲▲▲▲▲▲

CSI ELEMENTS: THE PERIODIC TABLE OF INVESTIGATIONS

Crime scene investigations and the field of forensic science rely on the properties of individual elements to illuminate (literally, in the case of the compound luminol) clues to crimes and to identify trace evidence left behind.

The element **osmium** has been used in fingerprint detection in the form of osmium tetroxide. When we touch a surface with our fingertips, we leave oils behind. Osmium reacts with the oils to form a black deposit that can be compared with the prints of a suspect.

Luminol uses a combination of elements (nitrogen, hydrogen, oxygen, and carbon) to detect the presence of another element, iron (present in the hemoglobin of blood). The compound is mixed with hydrogen peroxide and sprayed where investigators believe there may be traces of blood. The iron in blood acts as a catalyst between the hydrogen peroxide and the luminol compound, causing a reaction that emits photons and glows in a darkened room.

77 Ir IRIDIUM

Though rare in Earth's crust, iridium is much more plentiful in meteorites. After discovering thin layers of sedimentary rock with higher-than-usual concentrations of iridium throughout the world, scientists hypothesized that it was evidence of a meteor that caused the cataclysmic events that led to the extinction of non-avian dinosaurs 65 million years ago! Iridium's density, high melting point, and resistance to corrosion make it useful in alloys, but the lack of supply limits its use to pen tips, compass bearings, and spark plugs.

Category: Transition metal
Year discovered: 1803
Discovered by: Smithson Tennant, a British chemist
Fun fact: The largest meteorite ever to land in the United States, the Willamette Meteorite, contains much higher concentrations of iridium than is typically found on Earth.

Scientists theorize that an iridium-rich meteorite led to the extinction of some dinosaurs.

78 Pt PLATINUM

Platinum is the world's most prestigious element. Platinum is quite rare, though it is more abundant in Earth's crust than gold. Platinum is sought after for both its beauty and utility, and its market price reflects this demand.

▲ ▲

Not Just Sitting Pretty

Platinum has many superpowers, which contribute to its value. It is one of the few elements that resists simple acids and is resistant to high temperatures—so much so that it is difficult to melt. It is a beautiful silvery-white color and withstands tarnishing and corrosion: perfect for making jewelry. But platinum has other important jobs besides looking pretty. It is used as a catalyst for fuel cells that generate electricity or as catalytic converters in cars. Platinum is found in optical fibers, LCDs (liquid crystal displays) used in computer monitors and televisions, turbine blades, spark plugs, pacemakers, and effective cancer-eradicating drugs.

Platinum in spark plugs helps spark the ignition for the combustion needed to start a car.

GOLD

Gold is believed to be one of the first metals to be noticed and utilized by humans, which makes sense, as it can be found pure and rarely makes compounds in nature because it is one of the least reactive metals. It doesn't tarnish and retains both its golden color and shine forever, making it easy to distinguish from other elements. Its brilliance is immediate the moment you pick it up and dust it off.

Category: Transition metal

Year discovered: Approximately 4500 B.C.E.

Discovered by: Unknown

Fun fact: The largest single mass of gold was found in 1872 in the small town of Hill End in Australia and contained more than 198 pounds (90 kilograms) of gold.

The Gold Standard

Archaeologists have discovered that humans were making gold ornaments more than five thousand years ago. Its value and decorative use span centuries and civilizations. Gold's value is based on both its beauty and its rarity. Some have estimated that all the gold ever refined in history could fit into a cube with sides measuring 82 feet (25 metres).

Worth Its Weight

Most of the world's supply of gold—78 percent!— is used in jewelry, but gold is also a good conductor of electricity. Electrical contacts benefit from gold, as the connections never weaken by corrosion. Gold is used as a treatment for arthritis and in dental work as fillings and replacement teeth.

There's Gold in Them Thar Hills (and Oceans)!

Much of the gold is mined today with a process called gold cyanidation. Cyanide is used to leach the gold out of rock. Unfortunately, cyanide is toxic, and the process is dangerous to the environment. Less well known is the fact that our oceans are full of gold. In every cubic mile (1.6 cubic kilometre) of seawater there is 37 pounds (17 kilograms) of gold, but we have not yet found an economical way to recover it.

80 Hg MERCURY

Mercury is a fascinating element because of its mystifying and dangerous properties. It is the only metal element that remains liquid at room temperature. In fact, it freezes at –37.9° Fahrenheit (–38.8° Celsius) and doesn't boil until 674° Fahrenheit (357° Celsius)! When we refer to something as "mercurial," we are conjuring an image of the Roman god Mercury after whom the element was named. Mercury was both erratic and volatile and moved swiftly from place to place.

Category: Post-transition metal
Year discovered: Approximately 1500 B.C.E.
Discovered by: Unkown
Fun fact: Mercury is mostly found in the mineral cinnabar. The bright red compound mercury sulfide was used in cave paintings from 8000 to 7000 B.C.E. found in Turkey.

Mad as a Hatter

At one time people believed mercury prolonged life and induced good health. In reality it had the opposite effect and was poisoning the very people it was intended to help. The phrase "mad as a hatter" may have been coined to describe the demented behavior of hatmakers, who came into contact with mercury vapors in their work curing felt. Symptoms of mercury poisoning include personality changes, tremors, changes in vision, deafness, muscle incoordination, and difficulties with memory. Years later, scientists and the medical community began to understand that mercury was downright dangerous. In addition to causing damage to the brain, it is toxic to internal organs and the nervous system. Mercury poisoning was once quite common, but now it is rare due to health and safety regulations.

Fish in Troubled Waters

Toxic mercury enters our environment from the burning of fossil fuels (like coal) that infiltrate our air, water, and soil. In our oceans, mercury enters the marine food chain and the process of bioaccumulation begins: small fish that have just a little mercury in them are eaten by bigger fish that absorb all those bits of mercury, and the bigger fish are in turn eaten by bigger fish, and so on. With every marine meal, the mercury accumulates. Humans can enter this dangerous chain when we eat too much of certain species of fish that have high levels of mercury bioaccumulation like tuna or swordfish.

Careful Use

Mercury is still used in small amounts, but it is monitored carefully. Due to its density, mercury is used in some thermometers and barometers. A good conductor of electricity, it is still used widely in fluorescent bulbs and mercury vapor lamps.

81 Tl THALLIUM

Thallium is one of the toxic substances on the periodic table. Relatively abundant on Earth, it finds few uses because it is poisonous. Thallium sulfide is used in photocells, glass manufacturing, and medical scans.

▲ ▲

What's Your Poison?

By the mid-twentieth century, thallium had gained a reputation as the "poisoner's poison." Thallium sulfate, which was available as rat poison, was odorless, tasteless, and colorless, making it easy to slip into a victim's food or drink. The symptoms of vomiting, stomach pain, hair loss, and delirium that led to eventual death were confused for other conditions, masking the poisoner's weapon.

Category: Post-transition metal
Year discovered: 1861
Discovered by: William Crookes, a British chemist
Fun fact: Despite a toxic reputation, thallium was once used to treat ringworm and other skin infections.

82 Pb LEAD

Resistant to corrosion and easy to work with, lead has had many uses over the ages. One way that lead puts its powers to good use is as a shield against radiation, including in the lead apron you wear when you have dental or other medical X-rays.

Most of the element's uses were abandoned once we became aware of its toxicity. Our brains confuse lead for calcium and pump it to our neurons, causing serious cognitive and health issues. For decades, lead was added to gasoline to boost its effectiveness. The pollution this caused is a problem we are still trying to correct today. Many older homes have lead paint or lead solder in their pipes.

▲ ▲

Heavy Metal

Humans have been using lead for thousands of years. Ancient Egyptian tombs contain cosmetics made from lead compounds. Romans were some of the first people to use the element, mining 88,000 tons (80,000 tonnes) each year. The low melting point of the metal made it easy to weld and bend into pipes for running water systems. The Romans even sweetened their wine with lead. Some blame the fall of Rome on lead poisoning, hypothesizing that leaders fell prey to its deteriorating neurological effects.

Category: Post-transition metal
Year discovered: Ancient times
Discovered by: Unknown
Fun fact: The Latin word for lead is *plumbum*, which is the origin of both the abbreviation *Pb* and the word *plumber* (from the use of lead in pipes).

A lead apron protects your body from unnecessary radiation when you have an X-ray.

83 Bi BISMUTH

Since it is more abundant than other metals, bismuth was an important metal in the world of alchemy and was discovered by an unknown alchemist around 1500. Bismuth was often confused with lead and tin, and in 1753 Claude-François Geoffroy proved that it was a separate dense metal.

▲▲▲ ▲ ▲▲▲ ▲▲▲ ▲ ▲ ▲▲▲ ▲ ▲ ▲▲ ▲▲ ▲

Category: Post-transition metal
Year discovered: Approximately 1500
Discovered by: Unknown alchemist
Fun fact: Bismuth does not accumulate in the body like other heavy metals and is considered a safer alternative to lead for water pipes.

Tummy Soother

Since the eighteenth century, bismuth has been used in the treatment of stomach ailments. You may have ingested bismuth, as it is one of the active ingredients in Pepto-Bismol, the pink stuff you drink when you have an upset stomach or diarrhea. Its nontoxicity is quite extraordinary, considering that its direct neighbors on the periodic table are lead and polonium, both of which are extremely poisonous.

84 Po POLONIUM

Named for Marie Curie's native Poland, polonium is one of the most lethal substances known to man. Less than a microgram (about the size of a speck of dust) can kill you. Found in uranium ore and produced through nuclear reactions, it is rare due to its short half-life. Some applications of polonium involve harnessing its atomic power as a trigger in bombs.

Category: Post-transition Metal

Year discovered: 1898

Discovered by: Marie Curie, a Polish-French physicist

Fun fact: One of polonium's common isotopes is so radioactive that a solid lump of the extracted element will glow just by exciting the air around it.

▲ ▲

A Deadly Secret Agent

In 2006, Alexander Litvinenko, an ex-KGB officer, became violently ill after meeting two Russian men in a London hotel. He passed away after twenty-three agonizing days, and tests revealed significant amounts of polonium in his body. Because polonium is rare and difficult to obtain, the only possible source was a government with nuclear weapons.

RADIOACTIVE

85 At ASTATINE

With a half-life of a little more than eight hours, astatine exists in nature in the tiniest amounts—approximately 1 ounce (30 g) on the entire Earth at any given time. While created by the slow radioactive decay of uranium and thorium, astatine's half-life ensures that it has yet to find a biological role or human use, as it doesn't stick around for very long.

Category: Metalloid
Year discovered: 1940
Discovered by: Dale R. Corson and Kenneth Ross MacKenzie, American physicists, and Emilio Segrè, an Italian-American physicist

▲ ▲

86 Rn RADON

Radon has the distinction of being both the only radioactive noble gas and eight times heavier than air. It has few commercial uses because it causes cancer. Radon is formed from the decay of uranium and thorium in granite bedrock, so high concentrations of it exist in nature, but also in cities where granite is used to construct entire buildings. Gas escapes from the minerals inside granite into the air, and long-term inhalation can cause lung cancer. The amount of radon in the air is tiny, but it can be high near volcanic springs or geothermal power plants. There are high concentrations of radon in some people's basements, where it gets trapped because of a lack of airflow. A whole industry exists to detect and mitigate radon, including home test kits.

Category: Noble gas
Year discovered: 1900
Discovered by: Friedrich Ernst Dorn, a German physicist
Fun fact: Grand Central Terminal in New York City is made of granite. It is famously radioactive because it emits (a very small amount of) radon gas.

Granite rock

▲ ▲

87 Fr FRANCIUM

Francium, discovered in—you guessed it—France, has a half-life of twenty-two minutes. Highly radioactive and unstable, it has no commercial applications, as its time on Earth is fleeting. It is created for research purposes in a particle accelerator (a machine that uses electromagnetic fields to propel subatomic particles to high speeds) or nuclear reactor.

Category: Alkali metal
Year discovered: 1939
Discovered by: Marguerite Perey, a French chemist

FRANCE

88 Ra RADIUM

Radium compounds glow because radium's radioactivity causes emitted alpha particles to excite electrons in the other elements in the compound, and the electrons release their energy as light. The Curies discovered radium after isolating uranium from the mineral pitchblende and noticing that the remaining pitchblende was more radioactive than the isolated uranium. They realized that pitchblende must contain another radioactive element.

▲ ▲

Category: Alkaline earth metal
Year discovered: 1898
Discovered by: Pierre Curie, a French physicist, and Marie Curie, a Polish-French physicist
Fun fact: Marie Curie was enchanted by radium's luminescence (caused by its radioactivity) saying "the glowing tubes looked like faint fairy lights" in the workroom at night.

See the Light

In the early twentieth century, soon after its discovery, radium's luminescence and ability to kill cancer cells made it popular for both manufacturing (in glowing watch and clock dials) and as a cure-all tonic. Radium is a danger to more than cancer cells, and people who worked with radium in factories and health facilities began to fall ill. In the 1920s, women in factories who painted watch dials with the luminous radium paint, licking the brush between strokes as they were instructed, suffered debilitating health effects and even death. A group of the women sued their employers for damages, becoming known as the "radium girls." Their actions paved the way for better labor laws and safer work environments. While radium was put out of use, it had lasting health effects on those who came in contact with it, including Marie Curie. She died of aplastic anemia due to her exposure to radiation.

THE CURIES

....

Marie Skłodowska, born in 1867 in Warsaw, Poland, was an innovative and determined young scientist. She had transcended financial hardship, sexism, and political turmoil to pursue her passion for chemistry and physics when she met Pierre Curie, then a professor of physics, in Paris in 1894. Pierre would become both her husband and research partner. The pair immersed themselves in the study of radioactive elements, discovering polonium and radium after isolating them from the mineral called pitchblende. In 1903, they were awarded a Nobel Prize for their efforts, making Marie the first woman to receive the prize.

Tragically, Pierre was killed in an accident in 1906 when he fell under a horse-drawn cart while crossing the street, but Marie carried on their work alongside their daughter Irène. The two focused on radium's therapeutic uses for health and wellness. The damaging effects of radiation were not understood during Marie's lifetime, and she used few safety measures to protect herself. Her archive of papers, even her cookbook, are still radioactive to this day. Marie died of aplastic anemia in 1934, likely caused by exposure to radiation during her career of dedicated study, but her contributions to science live on as some of the most significant in history.

89 Ac ACTINIUM

Actinium is radioactive—it has a constant glowing blue halo. It exists in uranium ore, but most actinium is produced in nuclear reactors. While it has similar mechanical properties to lanthanum, because of its radioactivity it has not found many applications other than as an experimental radiation therapy for some cancers.

▲ ▲

Category: Actinoid
Year discovered: 1899
Discovered by: André-Louis Debierne, a French chemist

90 Th THORIUM

Unlike many of its fellow actinoids, thorium is abundant on Earth—seventy-six times more common than silver. It is no less radioactive than its fellow actinoids, however, and its wide availability made for some questionable uses (including in toothpaste!) before the full danger was understood. Scientists believe that eventually they can put thorium's abundance to good use in nuclear fission reactors to create electric power, but the start-up costs of additional research and operating challenges are high.

▲ ▲

Category: Actinoid
Year discovered: 1829
Discovered by: Jöns Jacob Berzelius, a Swedish chemist

91 Pa PROTACTINIUM

Protactinium means "before actinium," because uranium atoms decay to form protactinium atoms, which, in turn, break down into actinium. Accounting for 0.3 to 3.0 parts per million in uranium ores, protactinium is rare and difficult to produce. As a result, it has no practical applications beyond lab work by curious scientists.

Category: Actinoid
Year discovered: 1913
Discovered by: Kasimir Fajans, a Polish-American physical chemist, and Oswald Helmuth Göhring, a German chemist

92 U URANIUM

Uranium is the heaviest commonly found naturally occurring element. Refined uranium's toxic radioactivity and the destructive power of one of its isotopes has given it a well-deserved dangerous reputation. The first atomic bomb was powered by uranium. Given the incongruous nickname "Little Boy," it was dropped on Hiroshima in 1945, causing death, destruction, and devastating lasting effects on the environment and health of the citizens.

Category: Actinoid
Year discovered: 1789
Discovered by: Martin Heinrich Klaproth, a German chemist
Fun fact: The half-life of uranium-238 is 4.5 billion years, around the same age as Earth.

Fissile Out

Naturally occurring uranium is 99.27 percent uranium-238 and 0.72 percent uranium-235. Both of the isotopes are radioactive, but only the uranium-235 isotope is readily "fissile," meaning the nucleus, when bombarded by neutrons, can split and give off energy and more neutrons. This fission causes a chain reaction that powers the explosions in atomic weapons. It can also be harnessed and mediated in a nuclear reactor, which can power our homes and workplaces.

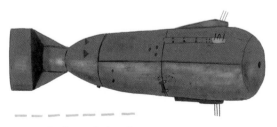

"Little Boy" atomic bomb

WHERE DO "HUMAN-MADE" TRANSURANIC ELEMENTS COME FROM?

The elements that come after uranium (numbers 93 and up) are called the transuranic elements, or sometimes the "human-made" or synthetic elements. We consider them human-made because they were not discovered naturally on Earth, but were produced through chain reactions in laboratories, although trace amounts of a handful of these elements, like neptunium and plutonium, have since been found on Earth. Synthetic elements are all radioactive and decay over time, transforming into lighter elements. For many of these elements, their half-lives are so short, compared to the age of Earth, that any of the atoms that may have existed when Earth formed 4.6 billion years ago have long since decayed.

But How Do Scientists "Make" an Element?

We know that an element is defined by and given the atomic number of the amount of protons it has in its nucleus (hydrogen has one proton and so on through the periodic table). So, to create a new element, we need to load up a nucleus with even more protons. Scientists were able to accomplish this by taking an isotope of uranium, U-238, and bombarding it with neutrons in a nuclear reactor until the nucleus of the atom became radioactive and converted its extra neutron into a proton, creating a new element. This method stopped working after fermium (element 100), and scientists instead

began colliding elements together in particle accelerators, trying to fuse the two nuclei of the atoms into one giant nucleus, creating new atoms altogether.

Are We Done Yet?

Scientists have thus far been able to cram 118 protons into a nucleus (the element oganesson), but the elements after 100 are so unstable that many last only milliseconds. As the density of the proton-packed nuclei increase, creating a stable element seems unlikely, but dedicated scientists are still making attempts at expanding the periodic table.

PARTICLE ACCELERATOR

A particle accelerator is a machine that speeds up elementary particles, such as electrons, protons, or atomic nuclei, to very high energies. Particle accelerators can be linear (in a straight line) or circular (in a circle). The first circular accelerator was shorter than 5 inches (12 centimetres), but scientists now work with accelerators that are 5 miles (8 kilometres) in diameter!

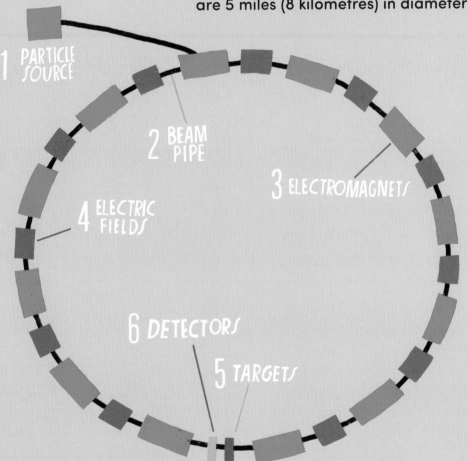

1 PARTICLE SOURCE

2 BEAM PIPE

3 ELECTROMAGNETS

4 ELECTRIC FIELDS

6 DETECTORS

5 TARGETS

1. Particle Source
Particles (electrons, protons, or atomic nuclei) start here.

2. Beam Pipe
The particles travel along in a vacuum (empty space where there is no matter, air, or other gas) inside this metal pipe.

3. Electromagnets
Electromagnets steer and focus the beam of particles.

4. Electric Fields
Electric fields switch from positive to negative energy at a given frequency to create radio waves that push and accelerate the particles.

5. Targets
Particles can be directed at a fixed target, or two beams of particles can be collided, which is how new elements are made.

6. Detectors
Particle detectors detect and record information about the particles and radiation that are produced by the collision.

93 NP NEPTUNIUM

Neptunium is one of the last of the actinoids that occurs naturally on Earth. That said, only trace quantities of neptunium are found in uranium ores, as it is formed by the radioactive decay of uranium into plutonium. Neptunium is used in neutron detectors.

Category: Actinoid
Year discovered: 1940
Discovered by: Edwin McMillan and Philip Abelson, American physicists

94 Pu PLUTONIUM

Plutonium is produced in nuclear reactors after a series of nuclear decays of uranium. At first, scientists were able to produce only scant amounts of plutonium that were invisible to the eye. The first visible amount weighed about three-millionths of a gram, but within years, Americans had amassed enough to power the "Fat Man" bomb dropped on Nagasaki in 1945.

Category: Actinoid
Year discovered: 1940
Discovered by: Glenn Seaborg and colleagues, American chemists
Fun fact: As a private citizen, it is illegal to possess plutonium. But there is one exception: a few people might have plutonium-powered pacemakers from the 1970s implanted in their bodies.

Risky Business

Two of plutonium's isotopes, plutonium-239 and plutonium-241, are fissile, which means they sustain a nuclear reaction. More than one-third of the energy produced in the world's nuclear reactors comes from plutonium. Plutonium waste is not only radioactive, but also toxic to humans if inhaled or ingested, collecting in the liver and bones. Because of its long half-life, plutonium waste will remain dangerous to humans for hundreds of thousands of years.

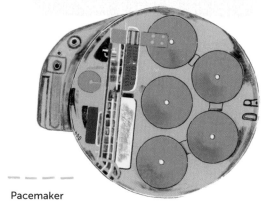

Pacemaker

RADIOACTIVITY

Crowded House

Radioactivity happens when a nucleus becomes overcrowded with nucleons (the protons or neutrons in a nucleus), causing the element to become unstable. Starting at polonium, all the elements that come after it on the periodic table are radioactive. When isotopes are unstable, they emit energy in the form of radiation through radioactive decay. Radiation can be deadly, penetrating our cells and causing cancer, but it can also be harnessed to target cancers and to generate energy. There are three types of radioactive decay: alpha, beta, and gamma. Alpha decay happens when a nucleus has too many protons or an unstable ratio of protons to neutrons and it emits a proton and a neutron, called an alpha particle, in an attempt to stabilize itself. Beta decay happens when there are too many neutrons in a nucleus, and it emits fast-moving electrons called beta particles. Gamma decay happens when there is too much energy in the nucleus, and it emits gamma rays, a high-energy form of light.

Living Your Best Half-Life

The half-life of a radioactive element is how long it takes for half the atoms to decay. In alpha and beta decay, an element's proton count transforms to a new element each time it decays. For example, uranium-238 decays through a chain of elements including thorium, protactinium, radium, radon, polonium, and bismuth, until it becomes the stable element lead. Elements with short half-lives are deadly because they are quick-acting, but those with long half-lives, such as those created in nuclear reactions, can pose long-term environmental hazards, as they decay over thousands of years.

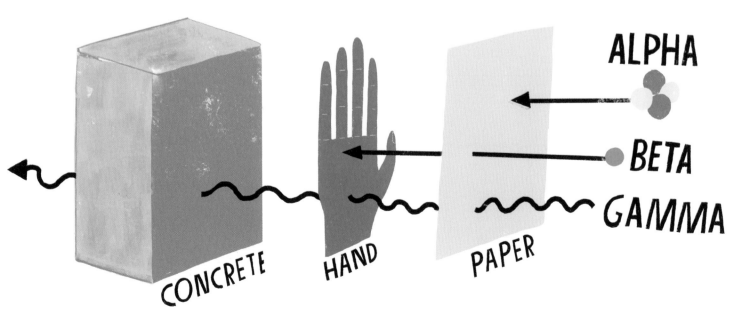

CONCRETE   HAND   PAPER

ALPHA

BETA

GAMMA

95 Am AMERICIUM

Americium is the one actinoid that you might find in your home. It is as radioactive as its cohorts, but in tiny amounts it can save lives. In household smoke detectors, a tiny gold-infused button of americium emits a radioactive stream that ionizes the air in a chamber and makes it conduct an electric current in the detector. If any smoke particles enter the chamber, they deionize the air, and the alarm is triggered.

Category: Actinoid
Year discovered: 1944
Discovered by: Glenn Seaborg and colleagues, American chemists

▲ ▲

96 Cm CURIUM

Any naturally occurring curium on Earth has long since decayed. Today it is only produced in nuclear reactors. Extremely radioactive, curium releases a lot of energy, but it is impractical to harness its energy because of its scarcity and the radioactive waste it creates. However, curium has been proposed for use to power spacecraft.

Category: Actinoid
Year discovered: 1944
Discovered by: Glenn Seaborg and colleagues, American chemists
Fun fact: The Curies did not discover curium, but it was named for them.

▲ ▲

⁹⁷Bk BERKELIUM

Berkelium is named for the place of its discovery: the University of California, Berkeley. Scientists bombarded an isotope of americium with alpha particles (the nucleus of helium) in a particle accelerator to produce a tiny sample of the element. Berkelium is not naturally occurring, and the amount of berkelium produced is tiny. Scientists don't know its boiling point, as they haven't acquired enough to measure it.

Category: Actinoid
Year discovered: 1949
Discovered by: Stanley Thompson, Albert Ghiorso, and Glenn Seaborg, American chemists

⁹⁸Cf CALIFORNIUM

Scientists first produced californium in a particle accelerator by bombarding curium with alpha particles at the University of California, Berkeley (and named it for the state). It is radioactive like the other actinoids, but californium has found some uses beyond research. It is a powerful neutron emitter that provides the spark to start a nuclear chain reaction in a nuclear reactor.

Category: Actinoid
Year discovered: 1952
Discovered by: Stanley Thompson, Kenneth Street Jr., Albert Ghiorso, and Glenn Seaborg, American chemists

99 Es EINSTEINIUM

Einsteinium was discovered in the fallout debris of the "Ivy Mike" bomb, the first nuclear explosion based on the principle of fusion (the uniting of atoms) rather than fission (the splitting of atoms). The research team that discovered the element decided to name it for German physicist Albert Einstein. It was Einstein's theory of relativity, summarized in the equation $E = mc^2$, that led to the understanding of nuclear chain reactions.

Category: Actinoid
Year discovered: 1952
Discovered by: Albert Ghiorso and colleagues, American chemists

100 Fm FERMIUM

Like einsteinium, fermium was discovered in the fallout debris of the "Ivy Mike" hydrogen bomb. Also like einsteinium, the element was named for a famous physicist, Enrico Fermi, an Italian-American pioneer in the field of nuclear physics. In 1942, Fermi built the first-ever fission reactor in a squash court at the University of Chicago.

Category: Actinoid
Year discovered: 1952
Discovered by: Albert Ghiorso and colleagues, American chemists

THE DEADLIEST ELEMENTS

Top prize goes to this triple threat. Like all the elements 84 and above, **plutonium** is radioactive, emitting dangerous alpha, beta, and gamma radiation. It is also toxic, particularly if inhaled. It is the material of choice for nuclear weapons.

It is its potential that makes **polonium** deadly. Just 0.03 ounces (1 gram) of polonium-210 could kill 10 million people.

A classic poison of detective novels, **arsenic**'s danger is no fiction. When ingested, it builds up in the body, causing gastric distress and eventual death.

Fluorine, the same element that helps protect our teeth, is toxic, corrosive, explosive, and lethal if inhaled.

Before we knew how toxic it was, **lead** was used in everything: paint, plumbing, toys, and even dinnerware. In high doses it is lethal, but even lower exposures are dangerous to children, permanently affecting their brain development.

ELEMENTS 101-118

We have reached the area of the periodic table where the elements do not have any practical use. Most have existed as a handful of atoms for a limited time, and many have not existed long enough or in sufficient quantities for chemical analysis. They were all human-made in particle accelerators and are often named for the scientists and locations associated with the labs that created them: the University of California, Berkeley; Lawrence Livermore National Laboratory; the Oak Ridge National Laboratory; the Joint Institute for Nuclear Research (JINR); the Institute of Physical and Chemical Research (RIKEN); and the Gesellschaft für Schwerionenforschung (GSI).

There are many contested claims on the discovery of humanmade elements, and depending on the source, you may see different dates or even different labs credited. We used the Royal Society of Chemistry for our attributions.

NAME	NUMBER	SYMBOL	CATEGORY	DISCOVERY DATE	PLACE OF DISCOVERY	NAMESAKE
MENDELEVIUM	101	Md	Actinoid	1955	UC Berkeley, USA	Dmitri Mendeleev, Russian chemist
NOBELIUM	102	No	Actinoid	1966	JINR, Russia	Alfred Nobel, Swedish chemist
LAWRENCIUM	103	Lr	Actinoid	1961	UC Berkeley, USA/ JINR, Russia	Ernest Lawrence, American physicist
RUTHERFORDIUM	104	Rf	Transition metal	1964	UC Berkeley, USA/ JINR, Russia	Ernest Rutherford, New Zealand physicist
DUBNIUM	105	Db	Transition metal	1968–70	UC Berkeley, USA/ JINR, Russia	Dubna, Russian town
SEABORGIUM	106	Sg	Transition metal	1974	Lawrence Berkeley National Laboratory	Glenn Seaborg, American chemist
BOHRIUM	107	Bh	Transition metal	1981	GSI, Germany	Niels Bohr, Danish physicist

HASSIUM	108	Hs	Transition metal	1984	GSI, Germany	German state of Hesse
MEITNERIUM	109	Mt	Unknown	1982	GSI, Germany	Lise Meitner, Austrian physicist
DARMSTADTIUM	110	Ds	Unknown	1994	GSI, Germany	Darmstadt, German city
ROENTGENIUM	111	Rg	Unknown	1994	GSI, Germany	Wilhelm Conrad Röntgen, German physicist
COPERNICIUM	112	Cn	Post-transition metal	1996	GSI, Germany	Nicolaus Copernicus, Polish astronomer
NIHONIUM	113	Nh	Unknown	2004	RIKEN, Japan	*Nihon*, the Japanese word for Japan
FLEROVIUM	114	Fl	Unknown	1999	JINR, Russia	Georgy Flerov, Russian physicist
MOSCOVIUM	115	Mc	Unknown	2003	JINR, Russia/ Lawrence Livermore National Laboratory, USA	Moscow, Russian city
LIVERMORIUM	116	Lv	Unknown	2000	JINR, Russia/ Lawrence Livermore National Laboratory, USA	Livermore, Californian city
TENNESSINE	117	Ts	Unknown	2010	JINR, Russia/ Lawrence Livermore National Laboratory, USA/ Oak Ridge National Laboratory, USA	Tennessee, American state and location of Oak Ridge National Laboratory
OGANESSON	118	Og	Unknown	2006	JINR, Russia/ Lawrence Livermore National Laboratory, USA	Yuri Oganessian, Russian nuclear physicist

STANDOUT CHEMISTS OF THE PERIODIC TABLE

When German-born scientist **Carl Wilhelm Scheele (1742–1786)** was fifteen years old, he apprenticed under a pharmacist in Sweden, where his knowledge of chemistry blossomed. Famed scientist Isaac Asimov referred to him as "hard-luck Scheele," because he discovered many elements for which other scientists are given credit, including oxygen, tungsten, barium, and hydrogen. Thankfully, he is given credit for discovering chlorine and molybdenum.

Martin Heinrich Klaproth (1743–1817) was a German chemist who discovered the elements uranium, zirconium, and cerium. He was an important German chemist of his time, writing more than two hundred papers and publishing a five-volume chemical dictionary.

British chemist **Sir Humphry Davy (1778–1829)** discovered or codiscovered barium, boron, calcium, magnesium, potassium, and sodium. As a young man, he was an apprentice to a surgeon, and in his spare time he taught himself chemistry, along with several other subjects, including theology, philosophy, poetry, and seven different languages!

One of the founders of modern chemistry, **Jöns Jacob Berzelius (1779–1848)**, was a Swedish chemist. He discovered selenium, silicon, cerium, and thorium. He is known for conducting pioneering experiments in electrochemistry (the study of the interaction between electrical energy and chemical processes), for being one of the first European scientists to accept atomic theory, and for recognizing the need for a new system of chemical symbols.

One of Jöns Jacob Berzelius's students was **Carl Gustaf Mosander (1797–1858)**. He discovered the elements lanthanum, erbium, and terbium. In 1832 he took over for Berzelius as professor of chemistry and pharmacy at the Karolinska Institute in Stockholm.

Sir William Ramsay (1852–1916) was a British chemist whose work in isolating the elements argon, helium, neon, krypton, and xenon led to the development of a new section of the periodic table: the noble gases. In 1904, he received the Nobel Prize in Chemistry.

Austrian physicist and close colleague of Berta Karlik, **Lise Meitner (1878–1968)** studied radioactivity and nuclear physics and discovered nuclear fission. She was the first woman to become a full professor of physics in Germany and later became the namesake of the element meitnerium.

German physicist and chemist **Ida Noddack (1896–1978)** discovered the element rhenium with her husband, Walter Noddack. For her work, she was nominated three times for a Nobel Prize. She was the first to propose the idea of nuclear fission in 1934.

Berta Karlik (1904–1990) was an Austrian physicist who discovered that astatine is a product of natural decay. Using her knowledge of both oceanography and radioactivity, she helped bring attention to the uranium contamination of seawater. She became the first female professor at the University of Vienna.

Marguerite Perey (1909–1975) was a French physicist and one of Marie Curie's students. She discovered the element francium. In 1962, she was the first woman to be elected to the French Académie des Sciences, an honor denied to her mentor Curie.

American chemist **Glenn Seaborg (1912–1999)** was intimately involved in the discovery of ten transuranic elements (chemical elements with atomic numbers greater than 92), which earned him a share of the 1951 Nobel Prize in Chemistry. His work led to his development of the arrangement of the actinoids series in the periodic table. The element seaborgium was named in his honor.

Albert Ghiorso (1915–2010) was an American nuclear scientist and the codiscoverer of a record twelve chemical elements on the periodic table: americium, curium, berkelium, californium, einsteinium, fermium, mendelevium, nobelium, lawrencium, rutherfordium, dubnium, and seaborgium.

Darleane C. Hoffman (b. 1926) is an American nuclear chemist who was among the researchers that confirmed the existence of seaborgium. She was part of the team who analyzed transuranic elements, making discoveries about the nature of fission that contributed to our knowledge of nuclear power. These elements decay quickly and typically exist for only short periods (see page 128).

American chemist **Dawn Shaughnessy (b. 1971)** leads the team at Lawrence Livermore Laboratory that discovered three new elements in 2016: elements 115, 117, and 118, called moscovium, tennessine, and oganesson. In total, she's helped discover six of the twenty-six elements added to the periodic table since 1940.

WOMEN OF THE PERIODIC TABLE

Women have been contributing to the discovery and understanding of the elements since the time of alchemy, but, unfortunately, many of their names and accomplishments have been lost to history. In the nineteenth and early twentieth centuries, as the scientific field of chemistry was established, women were discouraged from pursuing it as a career and were often allowed only secondary roles in laboratories. Marie Curie (read about her life and career on page 125) was a trailblazer for many and became a catalyst for change, although many women still struggle for recognition and opportunity in chemistry fields.

GLOSSARY

acid: A chemical substance that contains hydrogen and can react with other substances to form salts. When mixed with water, acids have a pH value of less than 7 and release the hydrogen as positive ions.

alchemy: A combination of scientific exploration and mysticism, concerned in particular with transforming common metals into gold. Practitioners of alchemy are called alchemists.

alkali: A substance with a pH value of more than 7. Alkalis form chemical salts when they are combined with acids.

allotrope: A different form of the same element. For example, allotropes of carbon are graphite, charcoal, and diamond. The different forms exist based on the different ways atoms may be bonded together.

alloy: A mixture of two or more metals or a metal and another element.

alpha particle: A helium nucleus (two protons and two neutrons) emitted by some radioactive substances.

antimicrobial: An agent that kills microorganisms like bacteria, fungi, and some viruses.

atom: An element in its smallest form, made up of protons and neutrons concentrated in the nucleus, around which electrons orbit.

atomic mass (or weight): A measure of the mass (weight) of an atom expressed as the sum of the total number of neutrons and protons in the nucleus.

atomic number: The number of protons in the nucleus of an atom.

atomic theory: The theory that all matter is made up of indivisible atoms.

boiling point: The temperature at which a substance starts to boil.

B.C.E.: Before Common Era: the Common Era begins with year one in our calendar.

catalyst: An element that facilitates a chemical reaction while itself remains unchanged.

catalytic convertor: A device that converts pollutants from engines into less toxic emissions.

compound: A substance that is made up of two or more chemically bonded elements.

core: The innermost layer of Earth's composition.

corrosion: The deterioration of a metal as a result of chemical reactions.

crust: The outermost layer of Earth's composition.

density: The physical property of matter that expresses a relationship of mass to volume. The more mass an object of a particular volume contains, the denser it is.

ductile: Describes a metal that can be stretched without losing its strength.

electric charge: The physical property that causes matter to experience a force when placed in an electromagnetic field.

electrolyte: A substance that carries electrical impulses.

electromagnetic force: A force between subatomic particles like protons and electrons that helps hold matter together.

electron: A subatomic particle with a net charge that is negative.

electron shell: Region of the atom where electrons are found. Atoms can have many different shells at varying distances away from the nucleus.

element: A substance that cannot be broken down further by chemical means, composed of atoms that have the same atomic number.

enzyme: A protein that speeds up chemical reactions.

ferromagnetic: A substance that has a high susceptibility to magnetization.

fiber optics: The thin, flexible glass or plastic fibers used to transmit light signals in telecommunication.

fission: A process by which the nucleus of an atom splits into smaller parts, releasing energy and free neutrons.

flammable: Easily set on fire.

fusion: A process by which the two light nuclei combine, forming a heavier element and releasing vast amounts of energy.

gamma radiation: Electromagnetic radiation emitted by the radioactive decay of atomic nuclei.

groups: The elements in a column of the periodic table. Elements in the same group have the same number of electrons in their outermost shell.

half-life: The time required for *half* the atoms of a given amount of a radioactive substance to decay into another element.

inert: A substance that is not chemically reactive.

ion: An atom or molecule in which there is an imbalance in the number of protons (positively charged particles) and electrons (negatively charged particles), resulting in a net electrical charge.

isotope: Forms of the same element that contain equal numbers of protons but different numbers of neutrons in their nuclei and therefore have a different atomic mass.

malleable: A substance's ability to be flattened or deformed under pressure.

mass: A measure of the amount of matter in an object.

metabolize: The process of a body breaking down a substance.

mineral: Naturally occurring (not human-made) crystalline solids that have a definite chemical composition.

molecule: Two or more chemically bonded atoms.

negative charge: The state of an atom or molecule with an extra electron or two.

neutron: A subatomic particle that has no net charge.

Nobel Prize: A set of annual international prizes awarded by Swedish and Norwegian institutions in recognition of academic, cultural, or scientific advances.

nuclear reactor: A machine used to generate energy through nuclear chain reactions.

nucleus: The dense center of an atom made up of neutrons and protons.

ore: A rock or mineral that contains metal.

organic matter: Material that comes from a recently living organism.

particle accelerator: A machine that uses electromagnetic fields to propel subatomic particles to high speeds.

periods: The rows of the periodic table that include elements that have the same number of electron shells in their atoms.

PGM: Platinum group metals—the densest and rarest metals on the periodic table including iridium, osmium, palladium, platinum, rhodium, and ruthenium.

pH scale: The measure of acidity (or basicity) of a solution, or its "potential of hydrogen."

polymer: A resilient substance composed of many repeated subunits.

positive charge: The state of an atom or molecule that has lost one or more electrons.

proton: A subatomic particle that has a positive charge.

radiation: Energy in the form of electromagnetic waves or subatomic particles.

radioactive decay: The process of an unstable atomic nucleus losing energy by emitting radiation.

reactive: The tendency of a substance to undergo a chemical reaction with another atom, molecule, or compound.

semiconductor: A solid substance that has electrical conductivity between an insulator and metal.

smelting: The process of heating ore to extract metal.

stable: The tendency of a substance to resist change or decomposition.

subatomic: Part of an atom or an action occurring within an atom.

transuranic elements: The elements with an atomic number greater than 92, which have a tendency to decay and transform into other elements.

valence electrons: The electrons in the outermost shell of an atom.

valence shell: The outermost electron shell of an atom.

volume: The quantity of three-dimensional space occupied by a liquid, solid, or gas.

INDEX

A
Abelson, Philip, 130
actinium, 21, 126, 127
actinoids, 18, 21
alchemy, 15
alkali metals, 18, 20
alkaline earth metals, 18, 20
alkalis, 20
allotropes, 28, 29
alloys, 12
alpha decay, 131
aluminum, 8, 39, 41, 52, 63
americium, 132, 141
ammonia, 30, 105
antimony, 8, 67, 93
antimony sulfide, 67
Arfwedson, Johan August, 25
argon, 48, 141
arsenic, 15, 63, 64, 72, 135
Asimov, Isaac, 138
astatine, 122
atomic clocks, 97, 107
atomic mass, 10, 18
atomic number, 10, 11, 18
atoms
    size of, 10, 11
    structure of, 10–11
ATP (adenosine triphosphate), 43
Auer von Welsbach, Carl, 100, 101, 107

B
Balard, Antoine-Jérôme, 74
barite, 98
barium, 98, 138
barium sulfate, 98
bauxite, 39
Berg, Otto Carl, 110
berkelium, 133, 141
beryllium, 26
Berzelius, Jöns Jacob, 42, 73, 99, 126, 141
beta decay, 131
bismuth, 120, 131
Black, Joseph, 37
Bohr, Niels, 136
bohrium, 136
borax, 27
boron, 27, 138
boron carbide, 27
boron nitride, 27
Brand, Hennig, 15, 43
Brandt, Georg, 63
brass, 12, 68
bromine, 44, 74
bronze, 68, 92
Bunsen, Robert, 77, 97

C
cadmium, 90, 94
calcium, 41, 50, 59, 78, 90, 119, 138
calcium carbonate, 50
calcium phosphate, 43, 50
calcium sulfate, 50
californium, 133, 141
carbon, 22, 28–29, 54, 59, 60, 111
carbon dioxide, 28, 33, 37
carbon monoxide, 87
catalytic converters, 86, 87, 88, 99, 113
Cavendish, Henry, 22
cellulose, 28
cerium, 99, 138, 139
cesium, 97
chemistry, history of, 15
chlorine, 12, 25, 46, 54, 59, 74, 138
chlorophyll, 37
chromium, 57, 59
chromium chloride, 57
chromium sesquioxide, 57
cinnabar, 116
Claude, Georges, 35
Cleve, Per Teodor, 24, 105, 106
cobalt, 59, 63, 102
cobalt arsenide, 63
cobalt oxide, 63
columbite, 81
compounds, 12–13
copernicium, 137
Copernicus, Nicolaus, 137
copper, 64, 66, 68, 69, 71, 89, 92, 94
copper carbonate, 68
Corson, Dale R., 122
Coryell, Charles D., 102
Coster, Dirk, 108
Courtois, Bernard, 95
Crawford, Adair, 78
Cronstedt, Axel Fredrik, 64
Crookes, William, 118
Cruickshank, William, 78
cupronickel, 64
Curie, Irène, 125
Curie, Marie, 121, 124, 125, 132, 140, 141
Curie, Pierre, 124, 125, 132
curium, 132, 141
cyanide, 115

D
Damascus steel, 56
darmstadtium, 137
Davy, Humphry, 27, 36, 49, 50, 98, 138
Debierne, André-Louis, 126
de Hevesy, George Charles, 108
Delafontaine, Marc, 105
del Rio, Andrés Manuel, 56
Demarçay, Eugène-Anatole, 103
diamonds, 28, 29
didymium, 100
dinosaurs, 112
Dorn, Friedrich Ernst, 122

dubnium, 136, 140
dysprosium, 104, 105

E
Earth
    crust of, 40–41
    magnetic field of, 60, 61
Einstein, Albert, 134
einsteinium, 134, 140
Ekeberg, Anders Gustav, 108
electrons, 10, 11
elements
    ancient concept of, 15
    categories of, 20–21
    collecting, 85
    deadliest, 135
    definition of, 9
    endangered, 53
    human-made, 9, 136–37
    in the Earth's crust, 40–41
    in the human body, 59
    number of, 9
    roles of, 8
    smelly, 44
    symbols for, 18, 66–67
    transuranic (human-made), 9,
        128, 136–37, 140, 141
Elhuyar, Fausto, 110
Elhuyar, Juan, 110
erbium, 106, 139
europium, 103, 104
europium oxide, 103

F
Fajans, Kasimir, 127
Fermi, Enrico, 134
fermium, 128, 134, 140
Flerov, Georgy, 137
flerovium, 137
flint, 42
fluoride, 34
fluorine, 34, 76, 135

fluorite, 34
Ford, Henry, 56
forensic science, 111
francium, 103, 123, 140
fuel cells, 22, 113
fullerene, 28, 29

G
Gadolin, Johan, 79
gadolinium, 104
Gahn, Johann Gottlieb, 58
gallium, 70
gamma decay, 131
gases, 14
Gay-Lussac, Louis-Josef, 27
Geoffroy, Claude-François, 120
germanium, 71
germanium dioxide, 71
Ghiorso, Albert, 133, 134, 140
Glendenin, Lawrence E., 102
global warming, 28
Göhring, Oswald Helmuth, 127
gold, 67, 88, 110, 113, 115
granite, 122
graphene, 28
graphite, 28, 29
Gregor, William, 54
groups, definition of, 19
Gutenberg, Johannes, 93
gypsum, 50

H
hafnium, 85, 108
half-life, definition of, 131
hassium, 137
Hatchett, Charles, 81
helium, 10, 22, 24, 53, 139
hemoglobin, 60, 111
Hisinger, Wilhelm, 99
Hjelm, Peter Jacob, 82
Hoffman, Darleane C., 141
holmium, 105

holmium oxide, 105
hydrobromic acid, 74
hydrochloric acid, 46
hydrofluoric acid, 34
hydrogen, 9, 11, 20, 22, 41, 59, 88,
    111, 138
hydrogen chloride, 46
hydrogen peroxide, 22, 111
hydrogen selenide, 44

I
indium, 53, 91
indium tin oxide (ITO), 91
iodine, 59, 95
ions, 11
iridium, 85, 112
iron, 40, 41, 60, 66, 111
iron oxide, 78
isotopes, 11

J
James, Charles, 107

K
Karlik, Berta, 140
Kirchhoff, Gustav, 77, 97
Klaproth, Martin Heinrich, 80, 99,
    127, 138
Klaus, Karl Karlovich, 84
Kroll process, 54
krypton, 35, 76, 139

L
Langlet, Nils Abraham, 24
lanthanoids, 18, 20, 53
lanthanum, 20, 99, 126, 139
Lavoisier, Antoine-Laurent, 45
Lawrence, Ernest, 136
lawrencium, 136, 140
lead, 67, 82, 90, 93, 94, 119, 120,
    131, 135